10/11

THE SZYK HAGGADAH

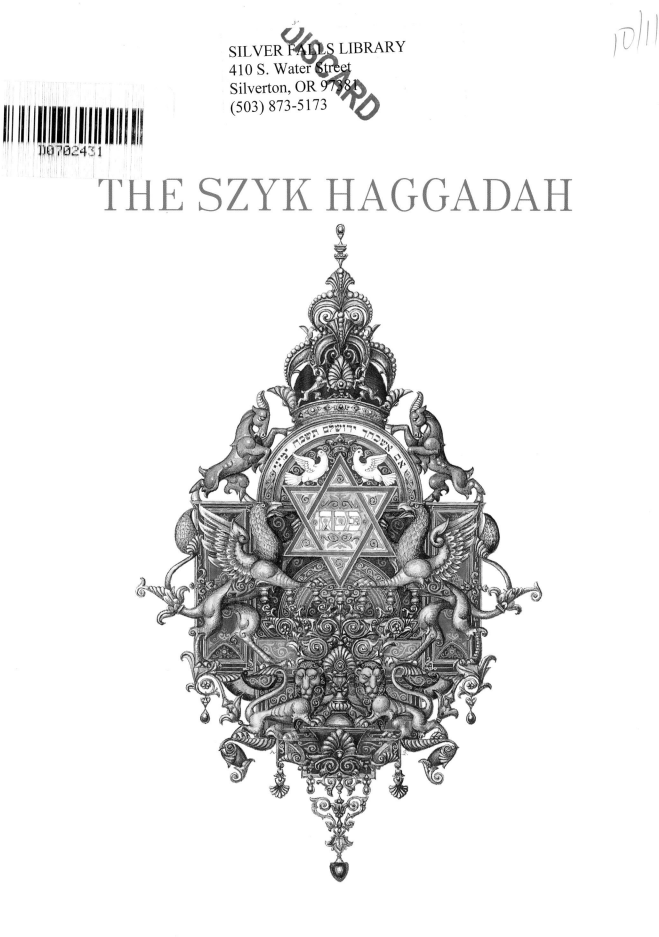

At the Feet of Your Most Gracious Majesty I Humbly lay these works of my hands, shewing forth the Afflictions of my People Israel

Arthur Szyk, illuminator of Poland.

Dieu et mon droit

THE HAGGADAH

ARTHUR SZYK

Translation and commentary by BYRON L. SHERWIN *with* IRVIN UNGAR

A HISTORICANA BOOK

ABRAMS, NEW YORK

PREPARING FOR PASSOVER

Passover commences before it begins—with arduous preparations. Passover does not just happen; it has to be "made." We refer to "making Passover."

Passover begins at home. It is a home-based festival. Weeks before the holiday begins, the task of making Passover commences with preparing the home. Every nook and cranny is cleansed, scrubbed, and dusted, with the kitchen getting special attention. All remnants of the elusive "antimatter" of Passover—ḥameitz, or leavened foods—are eventually removed, destroyed, and placed out of sight and out of mind for the duration of the holiday. The weeks and days before Passover are a time for giving charity to help ensure that the indigent have what they need, especially food, to properly observe the holiday.

As the night of the Seder approaches, the frenzy of preparation increases. Food for the festival needs to be acquired: food compatible with Passover laws and traditions, food untainted by leaven, foods traditionally eaten on Passover (which often differs, depending upon your family's place of origin). Pots, pans, plates, cups, and utensils are scoured and cleansed, with many people using different cooking and tableware than they use the rest of the year. Menus need to be thought out and eventually prepared.

But more than food needs to be prepared for the Seder. We should carefully consider whom to invite to help ensure that our Seders will be congenial and meaningful. At the Seder, each individual invited should be asked not only to attend but also to participate, depending on their abilities: to lead or sing a song, to read a prayer, to offer a commentary, to perform a short skit, to tell a story, to lead a game for the children, to discuss the meaning of freedom or liberation from oppression based on his or her own experience.

The Seder is both a food-fest and a talk-fest. The dining room is transformed into both a school and a synagogue: It becomes a place for learning, a sanctuary for prayer, and a salon for energized and meaningful conversation.

Each individual must also prepare spiritually for the observance. Passover is a time to contemplate how each of us can become liberated from that which enslaves, stifles, and inhibits each of us from realizing our own individual potential.

On the night before Passover, any remaining leaven is collected and then destroyed the next day in an age-old ritual (see next page). As the afternoon before Passover progresses, the table is set, the Seder plate is prepared, cooking proceeds, guests are welcomed. As the time for the Seder to begin approaches, festival candles are lit, seats are taken around the Seder table, and parents bless their children. With the recitation of *Kiddush*, the Seder commences. (For more on preparations for Passover, see Commentary, pages 13–14, 44–45.)

NOTE: The formatting of text in this Haggadah (the use of boldface print, italics, brackets, transliteration, etc.) is described in the Commentary, page 13.

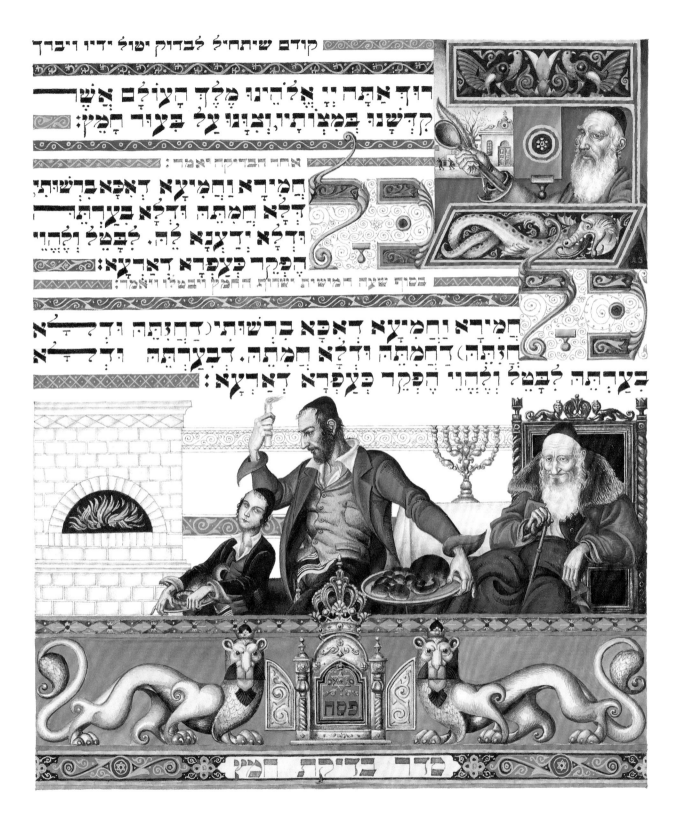

קודם שיתחיל לבדוק יטול ידיו ויברך

רוּךְ אַתָּה יְיָ אֱלֹהֵינוּ מֶלֶךְ הָעוֹלָם אֲשֶׁר
קִדְּשָׁנוּ בְּמִצְוֹתָיו,וְצִוָּנוּ עַל בְּעוּר חָמֵץ:

אחר הבדיקה יאמר :

חֲמִירָא וַחֲמִיעָא דְּאִכָּא בִרְשׁוּתִי,
דְּלָא חֲמִתֵּהּ וּדְלָא בְעַרְתֵּהּ,
וּדְלָא יְדַעְנָא לֵהּ. לִבָּטֵל וְלֶהֱוֵי
הֶפְקֵר כְּעַפְרָא דְאַרְעָא:

בשחרית אחר הביעור יאמר כל חמירא וחמיעא דאיכא ברשותי דחזתה ודלא חזתה וכו' יאמר:

חֲמִירָא וַחֲמִיעָא דְאִכָּא בִרְשׁוּתִי(דַּחֲזִתֵּי)וּדְלָא
חֲזִתֵּהּ)דַּחֲמִתֵּהּ וּדְלָא חֲמִתֵּהּ. דְּבַעַרְתֵּהּ וּדְלָא
בְעַרְתֵּהּ לִבָּטֵל וְלֶהֱוֵי הֶפְקֵר כְּעַפְרָא דְאַרְעָא:

סדר בדיקת חמץ

פסח

THE REMOVAL OF ALL LEAVEN

All leaven and products with leaven must be removed from the house during Passover (Exodus 12:15). The evening preceding the Seder, the house is searched for leaven (ḥameitz). In the eastern European Jewish tradition, this is done (as the illustrations depict) with a candle to see the leaven, a wooden spoon and a feather to help collect it, and a receptacle in which to place it. Today, many search with a flashlight, rather than a candle. Before beginning the search, a blessing in Hebrew and a legal formula in Aramaic are recited, declaring the leaven removed from one's possession. The following morning, before noon, the leaven is burned and the legal formula is recited again. For more on leaven and preparing the home for Passover, see Commentary, pages 13–14.

Before searching for the leaven (ḥameitz), this blessing, found in Hebrew on the right and translated and transliterated below, is recited:

Blessed are you, Lord our God, Sovereign of the Universe, who has sanctified us with his commandments, and has commanded us concerning the removal of leaven.

Barukh atah Adonai, Eloheinoo melekh ha-oh-lahm, asher kee-d'shah-noo b'meetz-voh-tav, v'tzee-vah-noo al bee-oor ḥameitz.

After inspecting the home for leaven, the following legal formula is recited:

Any leaven that may still be in my possession, whether I have noticed it or not, whether I have removed it or not, should now be considered as nonexistent, and ownerless like the dust of the earth.

Kol ḥamirah vah-ḥamee-ah d'ikka beer-shootee, d'lah ḥameetei oo-d'lah bee-artei, oo-d'lah y'da-nah lei, l'vah-teil v'leh-heh-vei hefkeir k'afrah d'ah-rah.

The following morning, not later than noon, the leaven collected the previous night is burned and declared nonexistent by reciting the legal formula above.

THE SEDER PLATE

The Talmudic rabbis required certain foods to be present on the dining table during the Passover Seder; however, they did not specify how they should be arranged there. Later on, placing these foods together on a "Seder plate" became standard practice. Various configurations for the items on the Seder plate were established, some including three *matzot* (plural of *matzah*) on the plate, but others placing the three *matzot* near the plate in a "*matzah* holder." No single configuration became standardized. The configuration depicted by Arthur Szyk on the right reflects the teachings of a school of Jewish mysticism, known as Lurianic kabbalah. Szyk superimposes a Star of David onto this configuration.

Beginning at the top of the star and going clockwise, these foods are: *matzot, z'roh-ah, ḥaroset, ḥazeret, karpas, bei-tzah, mah-rohr* (in the middle). For further discussion of the Seder plate and what should be on it, see Commentary, pages 15–17.

MATZOT. Passover is identified in Scripture as "The Festival of the *Matzot*" (e.g., Exodus 23:14, 34:18). *Matzah*, unleavened bread, is a reminder of the liberation from Egypt.

Z'ROH-AH, the shank bone, is a reminder of the Paschal sacrifice, which was discontinued once the Temple had been destroyed.

ḤAROSET. Not mentioned in the Bible with regard to Passover, *ḥaroset* is first mentioned in the Talmud (*Mishnah, Pesaḥim* 10:3). It is customary to dip the bitter herbs in the *ḥaroset*. There are different recipes for *ḥaroset*. A popular one contains wine, apples, nuts, honey, and cinnamon.

ḤAZERET is lettuce, probably romaine lettuce. It was originally used as the bitter herbs, since the leaves of the lettuce turned bitter as they ripened.

KARPAS is a leafy vegetable; often parsley is used. It is usually dipped in saltwater. This is a rabbinic tradition; it is not mentioned in the Bible.

BEI-TZAH is a hard-boiled or roasted egg, which serves as a reminder of the *Ḥagigah*, or festival sacrifice, offered at the Temple. It is customary to burn part of the egg's shell as a reminder of the destruction of the Temple through burning.

MAH-ROHR are the bitter herbs, which Szyk, following Lurianic tradition, places at the center of the plate. In some customs, the *ḥazeret* suffices for the bitter herbs. But, because the Talmud is unclear as to whether there should be both lettuce and other bitter vegetables on the table, a custom developed to place both there. Usually, grated horseradish root is used. Eating bitter herbs is a reminder of the bitterness of Egyptian slavery.

קַדֵּשׁ | וּרְחַץ | כַּרְפַּס

יַחַץ | מַגִּיד | רָחְצָה

מוֹצִיא | מַצָּה | מָרוֹר

כּוֹרֵךְ | שֻׁלְחָן עוֹרֵךְ | צָפוּן

בָּרֵךְ | הַלֵּל | נִרְצָה

קַדֵּשׁ

הִנְנִי מוּכָן וּמְזֻמָּן לְקַיֵּם מִצְוַת כּוֹס רִאשׁוֹן שֶׁל אַרְבַּע כּוֹסוֹת לְשֵׁם יִחוּד קֻדְשָׁא בְּרִיךְ הוּא וּשְׁכִינְתֵּיהּ עַל יְדֵי הַהוּא טָמִיר וְנֶעְלָם בְּשֵׁם כָּל יִשְׂרָאֵל:

THE ORDER OF THE SEDER

Seder means "order." Each of its fifteen steps is something we *do*, acts we perform.

Many people sing or recite the name of each step and those of previous steps before performing the next step. For example, before beginning the section called "Maggid," those present may intone: Kaddeish, Urḥatz, Karpas, Yaḥatz, Maggid.

At the bottom of the page to the right, which lists the parts of the Seder, Szyk adds a short *kavvanah* (plural: *kavvanot*), a mystical meditation; see Commentary, pages 42, 44.

1. **KADDEISH:** *Sanctify* the holiday by reciting *Kiddush*, the blessing over wine.

2. **URḤATZ:** *Wash* your hands, although without the blessing.

3. **KARPAS:** *Eat* a vegetable dipped in salt water, reciting the blessing before eating the vegetable.

4. **YAḤATZ:** *Break* the middle of the three matzot on the table. One part becomes the *Afikomen*.

5. **MAGGID:** *Tell* the story of Passover, from bondage to liberation, from oppression to freedom.

6. **ROHTZAH:** *Wash* the hands and say the blessing before eating.

7. **MOH-TZEE:** *Recite* the generic blessing over the food to be eaten during the Passover meal.

8. **MATZAH:** *Say* the blessing for the first eating of matzah during the Passover festival.

9. **MAH-ROHR:** *Eat* the bitter herbs after saying the blessing.

10. **KOH-REIKH** ("binding together"): *Make* and *eat* the "Hillel Sandwich," named after the great sage who established this tradition by "binding together" and eating *matzah* and bitter herbs dipped in *ḥaroset*.

11. **SHULḤAN OH-REIKH** ("set table"): *Enjoy* the festive meal at the "set table."

12. **TZAFOON** ("hidden"): *Find* and *eat* the "hidden" *matzah* or *Afikomen* that was set aside in *Yaḥatz*.

13. **BAREIKH:** *Recite* the Grace After Meals.

14. **HALLEIL:** *Recite* psalms and prayers of praise and gratitude to God.

15. **NEERTZAH** ("acceptance"): *Thank* God for the privilege of being able to celebrate the Seder, and *express* the hope that our worship is "accepted" by God, and that a complete and final redemption will soon be forthcoming.

Behold, I am ready and prepared to fulfill the commandment of drinking the first of the four cups of wine, for the sake of unifying the Blessed Holy One with his *Shekhinah* [The Divine Presence], which is hidden and mysterious, in the name of all Israel.

וַיְהִי עֶרֶב וַיְהִי בֹקֶר (בשבת מתחילין כאן)

הַשִּׁשִּׁי. וַיְכֻלּוּ הַשָּׁמַיִם וְהָאָרֶץ וְכָל צְבָאָם:
וַיְכַל אֱלֹהִים בַּיּוֹם הַשְּׁבִיעִי מְלַאכְתּוֹ אֲשֶׁר
עָשָׂה. וַיִּשְׁבֹּת בַּיּוֹם הַשְּׁבִיעִי מִכָּל מְלַאכְתּוֹ
אֲשֶׁר עָשָׂה. וַיְבָרֶךְ אֱלֹהִים אֶת יוֹם הַשְּׁבִיעִי וַיְקַדֵּשׁ אֹתוֹ כִּי
בוֹ שָׁבַת מִכָּל מְלַאכְתּוֹ אֲשֶׁר בָּרָא אֱלֹהִים לַעֲשׂוֹת:

סַבְרִי מָרָנָן וְרַבָּנָן וְרַבּוֹתַי (בחול מתחילין כאן)

אַתָּה יְיָ אֱלֹהֵינוּ מֶלֶךְ הָעוֹלָם בּוֹרֵא פְּרִי
הַגָּפֶן:

אַתָּה
יְיָ
אֱלֹהֵינוּ
מֶלֶךְ
הָעוֹלָם
אֲשֶׁר בָּחַר בָּנוּ מִכָּל עָם. וְרוֹמְמָנוּ
מִכָּל לָשׁוֹן
וְקִדְּשָׁנוּ בְּמִצְוֹתָיו. וַתִּתֶּן לָנוּ יְיָ אֱלֹהֵינוּ
בְּאַהֲבָה (לשבת
שַׁבָּתוֹת לִמְנוּחָה וּ) מוֹעֲדִים לְשִׂמְחָה חַגִּים וּזְמַנִּים
לְשָׂשׂוֹן (אֶת יוֹם הַשַּׁבָּת הַזֶּה וְ) אֶת יוֹם חַג הַמַּצּוֹת הַזֶּה

THE SEDER BEGINS

KADDEISH (*Kiddush*/sanctification)

Unlike *matzah* and bitter herbs, Scripture nowhere requires drinking wine at the Seder. However, to satisfy the biblical obligation to rejoice on the festival, the Talmudic rabbis required the drinking of wine at the Seder. Affirming an already extant custom, they specifically required drinking four cups of wine (*Mishnah, Pesaḥim* 10:1), the first of which is the wine of *Kiddush*, a blessing on the occasion of the festival day. On wine and Passover, see Commentary, page 18.

Fill each wine cup. This is the first of four cups of wine we drink at the Seder. In some homes, children are given grape juice rather than wine. Some fill the children's cups with candy instead of wine.

(On the Sabbath—Friday evening—begin here):

"And there was evening and there was morning, the sixth day. The heavens and the earth and all that they contained were finished. On the seventh day [the Sabbath], God completed the work that he had been doing; God rested on the seventh day from all the work that he had done. God blessed the seventh day and hallowed it, because on it he rested from all the work of creation that he had made" (Genesis 1:31–2:3).

On weekdays, begin here:

Blessed are you, Lord our God, Sovereign of the Universe, who creates the fruit of the vine.

Barukh atah Adonai, Eloheinoo melekh ha-oh-lahm, boh-rei p'ree ha-gah-fen.

On the Sabbath, add the words in parentheses:

Blessed are you, Lord our God, Sovereign of the Universe, who has chosen us from among all peoples, who has exalted us from among those who speak other tongues, and who has sanctified us with his commandments. You, Lord our God, have given us with love (Sabbath days for rest and) festivals for joy, holydays and festive seasons for rejoicing on (this Sabbath day as well as) this Festival of the **Matzot**—[continued on the next page]

זְמַן חֵרוּתֵנוּ (בְּאַהֲבָה) מִקְרָא קֹדֶשׁ זֵכֶר לִיצִיאַת
מִצְרָיִם. כִּי בָנוּ בָחַרְתָּ וְאוֹתָנוּ קִדַּשְׁתָּ מִכָּל הָעַמִּים
(וְשַׁבָּת) וּמוֹעֲדֵי קָדְשֶׁךָ (בְּאַהֲבָה וּבְרָצוֹן) בְּשִׂמְחָה
וּבְשָׂשׂוֹן הִנְחַלְתָּנוּ. בָּרוּךְ אַתָּה יְיָ מְקַדֵּשׁ (הַשַּׁבָּת) יִשְׂרָאֵל
וְהַזְּמַנִּים:

(בְּמוֹצָאֵי שַׁבָּת אוֹמְרִים)

בָּרוּךְ אַתָּה יְיָ אֱלֹהֵינוּ מֶלֶךְ הָעוֹלָם בּוֹרֵא מְאוֹרֵי הָאֵשׁ:

אַתָּה יְיָ אֱלֹהֵינוּ מֶלֶךְ הָעוֹלָם הַמַּבְדִּיל בֵּין קֹדֶשׁ לְחֹל בֵּין אוֹר לְחֹשֶׁךְ
בֵּין יִשְׂרָאֵל לָעַמִּים. בֵּין יוֹם הַשְּׁבִיעִי לְשֵׁשֶׁת יְמֵי הַמַּעֲשֶׂה. בֵּין קְדֻשַּׁת
שַׁבָּת לִקְדֻשַּׁת יוֹם טוֹב הִבְדַּלְתָּ. וְאֶת יוֹם הַשְּׁבִיעִי מִשֵּׁשֶׁת יְמֵי הַמַּעֲשֶׂה
קִדַּשְׁתָּ. הִבְדַּלְתָּ וְקִדַּשְׁתָּ אֶת עַמְּךָ יִשְׂרָאֵל בִּקְדֻשָּׁתֶךָ: בָּרוּךְ אַתָּה יְיָ הַמַּבְדִּיל בֵּין קֹדֶשׁ לְקֹדֶשׁ

בָּרוּךְ אַתָּה יְיָ אֱלֹהֵינוּ מֶלֶךְ הָעוֹלָם שֶׁהֶחֱיָנוּ וְקִיְּמָנוּ
וְהִגִּיעָנוּ לַזְּמַן הַזֶּה:

וְרָחַץ כַּרְפַּס יַחַץ מַגִּיד

נוֹטֵל יָדָיו וּבְלִי בְּרָכָה לוֹקֵחַ כַּרְפַּס פָּחוֹת וּבֹצֵעַ מַצָּה שְׁנִיָּה וְיָנִיחַ מְגַלִּין הַמַּצָּה וְנוֹטְלִין וּבִצַּע
נְטִילַת יָדָיִם מִכְּזַיִת וְיִטְבּוֹל בְּמֵי חֲצִיָּה הַקְּטַנָּה בִּמְקוֹמָהּ וְהַדֵּעַ מַעֲלֵי הַקְּעָרָה וּמַגְבִּיהִין
מֶלַח אוֹ בַּחוֹמֶץ וִיבָרֵךְ וְהַגְּדוֹלָה יִצְפֹּן לְאָפִיקוֹמָן אוֹ תְהֹא אוֹמְרִין הָא לַחְמָא קּלָם

בָּרוּךְ אַתָּה יְיָ אֱלֹהֵינוּ מֶלֶךְ הָעוֹלָם בּוֹרֵא פְּרִי הָאֲדָמָה

הִנְנִי מוּכָן וּמְזֻמָּן לְקַיֵּם הַמִּצְוָה לְסַפֵּר בִּיצִיאַת מִצְרַיִם לְשֵׁם יִחוּד קֻדְשָׁא בְּרִיךְ הוּא וּשְׁכִינְתֵּיהּ עַל יְדֵי הַהוּא
טָמִיר וְנֶעְלָם בְּשֵׁם כָּל יִשְׂרָאֵל:

the season of our freedom (with love). It is a holy convocation, in memory of the Exodus from Egypt. For you have chosen us, and you have sanctified us, from among all peoples. You have bestowed upon us (the Sabbath and) the sacred festivals (with love and desire), with gladness and joy. Blessed are you, Lord, who hallows (the Sabbath,) the people of Israel, and the festive seasons.

On Saturday night, to conclude the Sabbath, light a havdalah *candle (note that spices are not used as they are on most Saturday nights) and say these blessings:*

Blessed are you, Lord our God, Sovereign of the Universe, who creates the light of the fire.

Blessed are you, Lord our God, Sovereign of the Universe, who has set a distinction between the holy and the ordinary, light and darkness, the people of Israel and other peoples, the Sabbath and the six days of creation. You, God, have further distinguished between the sanctity of the Sabbath and that of the festivals; you distinguish and sanctify your people Israel with your holiness. Blessed are you Lord, who makes a distinction between these [two] varieties of holiness [—the holiness of the Sabbath and that of the festivals].

On all nights continue:

Blessed are you, Lord our God, Sovereign of the Universe, who has kept us in life, who has sustained us, and who has enabled us to reach this occasion.

Barukh atah Adonai, Eloheinoo melekh ha-oh-lahm, sheh-heh-ḥee-yah-noo, v'kee-yem-ah-noo, v'hee-gee-yah-noo lah-z'mahn ha-zeh.

Now, everyone drinks from the first cup of wine while reclining. Each of the four cups should be fully emptied or almost emptied, and not merely sipped.

NOTE: On the bottom of the facing page to the right, Szyk depicts and gives instructions regarding the next four parts of the Seder. The first of the four is given here; the others are discussed on the next page.

URḤATZ

For this second part of the Seder, the hands are washed without saying a blessing. In some homes, it is customary for only the leader of the Seder to wash his or her own hands. In others, someone takes a cup and a bowl of water around the table and pours the water over the hands of each participant. It is customary to pour water over each hand two or three times, placing a bowl underneath to catch the water.

וירא והנה שלשה אנשים נצבים עליו

הָא לַחְמָא עַנְיָא דִּי אֲכָלוּ אַבְהָתָנָא בְּאַרְעָא דְמִצְרַיִם. כָּל דִּכְפִין יֵיתֵי וְיֵיכֹל, כָּל דִּצְרִיךְ יֵיתֵי וְיִפְסַח. הָשַׁתָּא הָכָא, לְשָׁנָה הַבָּאָה בְּאַרְעָא דְיִשְׂרָאֵל. הָשַׁתָּא עַבְדֵי, לְשָׁנָה הַבָּאָה בְּנֵי חוֹרִין.

KARPAS

For this third part of the Seder, each person takes a piece of karpas, *a leafy green vegetable, usually parsley, measuring less than the volume of half an egg, and dips it into saltwater (symbolizing the splitting of the Sea of Reeds) or vinegar (symbolizing the tears of the enslaved Israelites), and he or she says:*

Blessed are you, Lord our God, Sovereign of the Universe, who creates the fruit of the earth.

בָּרוּךְ אַתָּה יהוה אֱלֹהֵינוּ מֶלֶךְ הָעוֹלָם בּוֹרֵא פְּרִי הָאֲדָמָה:

Barukh atah Adonai, Eloheinoo melekh ha-oh-lahm, boh-rei p'ree ha-ah-dah-mah.

The vegetable serves as a kind of hors d'oeuvre. At this point, some serve other light hors d'oeuvres, especially to hungry children.

YAḤATZ

For the fourth part of the Seder, one breaks the middle matzah *of the three* matzot *and replaces the smaller piece, while the larger piece is set aside for the* Afikomen.

MAGGID

Maggid is the fifth part of the Seder, and focuses on telling the story of Passover. It is the most lengthy and central part of the Seder, which is fitting since it deals with the central purpose of the Seder: telling, interpreting and conveying the story of Passover, the story of the bondage in Egypt and of the Exodus. On how the rabbis taught that the story should be told in the Haggadah, and on the symbolism of *matzah*, see Commentary, pages 17, 18–25.

Maggid *begins with an invitation to the hungry and needy to join us at the Seder. As we invite the needy to our Seder, it is customary to open the front door while reciting or singing the Aramaic text on the facing page. The* matzah *is uncovered and is shown. Some remove the egg and shank bone from the Seder plate and raise the plate.*

This is the bread of affliction that our ancestors ate in the Land of Egypt. Let all who are hungry, enter and eat. Let all who are in need, come in to celebrate Passover. Now, we are here. Next year, we shall be in the Land of Israel. Now, we are enslaved. Next year, we shall be free.

Ha laḥ-ma ahn-yah dee ah-khal-oo av-ha-ta-na b'ahr-ah d'mitz-rayeem. Kohl deekh-feen yei-tei v'yei-khol, kohl deetz-reekh yei-tei v'yeefsaḥ. Ha-shata ha-khah, l'shanah ha-ba-ah b'ahr-ah d'yisraeil. Ha-shata ahv-dei l'shanah ha-ba-ah b'nei ḥoreen.

נִשְׁתַּנָּה הַלַּיְלָה הַזֶּה מִכָּל הַלֵּילוֹת. שֶׁבְּכָל הַלֵּילוֹת אָנוּ אוֹכְלִין חָמֵץ וּמַצָּה הַלַּיְלָה הַזֶּה כֻּלּוֹ מַצָּה. שֶׁבְּכָל הַלֵּילוֹת אָנוּ אוֹכְלִין שְׁאָר יְרָקוֹת הַלַּיְלָה

הַזֶּה מָרוֹר. שֶׁבְּכָל הַלֵּילוֹת אֵין אָנוּ מַטְבִּילִין אֲפִלּוּ פַּעַם אַחַת, הַלַּיְלָה הַזֶּה שְׁתֵּי פְעָמִים. שֶׁבְּכָל הַלֵּילוֹת אָנוּ אוֹכְלִין בֵּין יוֹשְׁבִין וּבֵין מְסֻבִּין, הַלַּיְלָה הַזֶּה כֻּלָּנוּ מְסֻבִּין

THE FOUR QUESTIONS

The "telling" of the Passover narrative does not begin with the story or even with the person who tells it, but with questions and the person who asks them. The unusual features of the Passover meal, such as the items placed on the Seder plate and the rituals performed at the Seder, are meant to stimulate and to evoke questions and curiosity, especially from the children who are present. Until the question is asked, the story cannot be told. Until the child inquires, the parent cannot discharge his or her obligation to answer the child by telling the story and explaining its meaning (Exodus 13:14). On the Four Questions, their origin, their meaning, and textual variants, see Commentary, pages 27–28.

Beginning in medieval times, it became customary for the youngest child to ask the Four Questions. But, because Judaism teaches that learning is a lifelong process, the Talmudic rabbis insisted that even if two scholars celebrate the Seder only with one another, they should nonetheless pose, answer, and discuss these questions (*Talmud, Pesaḥim* 116a).

Why is this night different from all other nights?:
On all other nights, we eat either leaven or *matzah*. Why, on this night, do we eat only *matzah*?

On all other nights, we eat all types of vegetables. Why, on this night, must we specifically eat bitter herbs?

On all other nights, we do not dip [vegetables] even once. Why, on this night, do we dip twice?

On all other nights, we eat either sitting upright or reclining. Why, on this night, do we all eat reclining?

Mah neesh-tah-nah ha-ly-lah ha-zeh mee-kohl ha-lei-loht.

Sheh-b'khowl ha-lei-loht ah-noo oh-khleen ḥameitz oo-matzah, ha-ly-lah ha-zeh, koo-loh matzah.

Sheh-b'khowl ha-lei-loht ah-noo oh-khleen sh'ohr yeer-ah-koht, ha-ly-lah ha-zeh mah-rohr.

Sheh-b'khowl ha-lei-loht ein ah-noo maht-bee-leen ah-fee-loo pah-ahm eh-ḥaht, ha-ly-lah ha-zeh, sh'tei p'ah-meem.

Sheh-b'khowl ha-lei-loht ah-noo oh-khleen bein yosh-veen oo-vein m'soo-been, ha-ly-lah ha-zeh koo-lah-noo m'soo-been.

בָדִים הָיִינוּ לְפַרְעֹה בְּמִצְרַיִם
וַיּוֹצִיאֵנוּ יְיָ אֱלֹהֵינוּ מִשָּׁם בְּיָד
חֲזָקָה וּבִזְרוֹעַ נְטוּיָה . וְאִלּוּ לֹא
הוֹצִיא הַקָּדוֹשׁ בָּרוּךְ הוּא אֶת
אֲבוֹתֵינוּ מִמִּצְרַיִם, הֲרֵי אָנוּ
וּבָנֵינוּ וּבְנֵי בָנֵינוּ מְשֻׁעְבָּדִים
הָיִינוּ לְפַרְעֹה בְּמִצְרָיִם. וַאֲפִילוּ
כֻּלָּנוּ חֲכָמִים. כֻּלָּנוּ נְבוֹנִים.
כֻּלָּנוּ זְקֵנִים. כֻּלָּנוּ יוֹדְעִים אֶת
הַתּוֹרָה . מִצְוָה עָלֵינוּ לְסַפֵּר
בִּיצִיאַת מִצְרַיִם. וְכָל הַמַּרְבֶּה
לְסַפֵּר בִּיצִיאַת מִצְרַיִם הֲרֵי
זֶה מְשֻׁבָּח:

מֹשֶׁה וְאַהֲרֹן לִפְנֵי פַרְעֹה

WE WERE SLAVES

How do we tell the Passover story? This is the question that confronted the Talmudic rabbis after the destruction of the Temple, and that has confronted every generation since. The rabbis enjoined us at the Seder to tell the story by "beginning with shame and degradation and ending with praise" for redemption. But, the rabbis debated what it means to begin with shame and degradation (*Talmud, Pesaḥim* 116a). One view, expressed in the paragraph that follows, is that "shame" refers to the physical degradation of slavery in Egypt. This movement from shame to praise, from degradation to glory, and from the threat of annihilation to the exhilaration of redemption, is discussed throughout the Haggadah. For further information, see Commentary, pages 20–22.

"We were slaves to Pharaoh in Egypt, but the Lord, our God, took us out of there with a mighty hand" and an outstretched arm (Deuteronomy 6:21). If the Blessed Holy One had not taken our ancestors out of Egypt, then we, and our children, and their descendants, might still be enslaved to Pharaoh in Egypt. Now, even were all of us scholars, wise, and learned in the Torah, we would still be obliged to tell the story of the Exodus from Egypt. Moreover, whosoever elaborates upon the story of the Exodus from Egypt is praiseworthy.

Some sing a version of this text in Hebrew:

Avah-deem ha-yee-noo, ha-yee-noo, atah b'nei ḥoreen, b'nei ḥoreen. Avah-deem, ha-ha-yee-noo, atah, atah, b'nei ḥoreen, b'nei ḥoreen.

בְּרַבִּי אֱלִיעֶזֶר וְרַבִּי יְהוֹשֻׁעַ וְרַבִּי אֶלְעָזָר
בֶּן עֲזַרְיָה וְרַבִּי עֲקִיבָא וְרַבִּי טַרְפוֹן
שֶׁהָיוּ מְסֻבִּין בִּבְנֵי בְרַק וְהָיוּ מְסַפְּרִים
בִּיצִיאַת מִצְרַיִם כָּל אוֹתוֹ הַלַּיְלָה עַד שֶׁ...אוּ
תַלְמִידֵיהֶם וְאָמְרוּ לָהֶם. רַבּוֹתֵינוּ הִגִּיעַ זְמַן קְרִיאַת שְׁמַע שֶׁל שַׁחֲרִית:

אָמַר רַבִּי אֶלְעָזָר בֶּן עֲזַרְיָה. הֲרֵי אֲנִי כְּבֶן שִׁבְעִים שָׁנָה וְלֹא זָכִיתִי
שֶׁתֵּאָמֵר יְצִיאַת מִצְרַיִם בַּלֵּילוֹת. עַד שֶׁדְּרָשָׁהּ בֶּן זוֹמָא. שֶׁנֶּאֱמַר לְמַעַן תִּזְכֹּר
אֶת יוֹם צֵאתְךָ מֵאֶרֶץ מִצְרַיִם כָּל יְמֵי חַיֶּיךָ. יְמֵי חַיֶּיךָ הַיָּמִים. כָּל יְמֵי חַיֶּיךָ
הַלֵּילוֹת. וַחֲכָמִים אוֹמְרִים. יְמֵי חַיֶּיךָ הָעוֹלָם הַזֶּה. כָּל יְמֵי חַיֶּיךָ לְהָבִיא לִימוֹת
הַמָּשִׁיחַ:

Continuing the theme of the importance of telling the Passover story, and reflecting the statement of the previous paragraph that obliges even scholars to tell, study, and discuss the story, two tales about scholars doing precisely that are now recounted. The first is of unknown origin, while the second derives from an early rabbinic text (*Mishnah*, *Berakhot* 1:5). This text reflects the rabbinic view that, at the Seder, one is not only required to feast, but also to study. How various biblical verses are to be interpreted as they relate to Passover, and even legal issues regarding Passover, are included in these studies at the Seder. For example, the following reflects a legal debate over the question of whether the third paragraph of the *Shema* that refers to the liberation from Egypt (Numbers 15:37–41) should be recited only in the morning; or, should it also be recited at night as part of the evening liturgy? If only in the morning, then how could the story of the Exodus be told in the evening when the Seder is held? The rabbis ruled that the Passover story could be mentioned in the evening, making the Seder, which takes place in the evening, possible. For further discussion, see Commentary, pages 25–27.

And so it happened that Rabbi Eliezer, Rabbi Joshua, Rabbi Eleazar ben Azariah, Rabbi Akiva, and Rabbi Tarfon were gathered together [to celebrate Passover] at [the town of] B'nai Brak, where they reclined [as is customary at the Seder], and spoke about the Exodus from Egypt the entire night. In the morning [as they were still discussing the meaning of the Exodus], their disciples arrived and said to them, "Our masters, the time has arrived to recite the *Shema* prayer of the morning."

Rabbi Eleazar ben Azariah said, "Though I am like a seventy-year-old man, until Ben Zoma explained it, I had never been able to understand why the story of the Exodus from Egypt is recited in the evening. As it is written, 'so that you may remember the day of your exodus from Egypt all the days of your life' (Deuteronomy 16:3). [As Ben Zoma explained,] Had the verse only said, 'the days of your life,' it would have meant only the days [and not also the nights]. But, because it is written, '*all* the days of your life,' it refers to the nights [as well as to the days]." But, the other sages interpreted the verse [differently than Ben Zoma]: "Had only 'the days of your life' been written, it would have referred only to life in this world, but because the verse reads '*all* the days of your life,' it refers [not only to life in this world but] also to life in the future days of messianic redemption [called 'the World-to-Come']."

חָכָם מַה הוּא אוֹמֵר. מָה הָעֵדֹת וְהַחֻקִּים וְהַמִּשְׁפָּטִים אֲשֶׁר צִוָּה יְיָ אֱלֹהֵינוּ אֶתְכֶם. וְאַף אַתָּה אֱמָר לוֹ כְּהִלְכוֹת הַפֶּסַח אֵין מַפְטִירִין אַחַר הַפֶּסַח אֲפִיקוֹמָן:

הַמָּקוֹם. בָּרוּךְ הוּא. בָּרוּךְ שֶׁנָּתַן תּוֹרָה לְעַמּוֹ יִשְׂרָאֵל. בָּרוּךְ הוּא. כְּנֶגֶד אַרְבָּעָה בָנִים דִּבְּרָה תוֹרָה. אֶחָד חָכָם. וְאֶחָד רָשָׁע. וְאֶחָד תָּם. וְאֶחָד שֶׁאֵינוֹ יוֹדֵעַ לִשְׁאוֹל:

רָשָׁע מַה הוּא אוֹמֵר. מָה הָעֲבוֹדָה הַזֹּאת לָכֶם. לָכֶם וְלֹא לוֹ. וּלְפִי שֶׁהוֹצִיא אֶת עַצְמוֹ מִן הַכְּלָל כָּפַר בְּעִקָּר. וְאַף אַתָּה הַקְהֵה אֶת שִׁנָּיו וֶאֱמָר לוֹ. בַּעֲבוּר זֶה עָשָׂה יְיָ לִי בְּצֵאתִי מִמִּצְרָיִם. לִי וְלֹא לוֹ. אִלּוּ הָיָה שָׁם לֹא הָיָה נִגְאָל:

תָּם מַה הוּא אוֹמֵר. מַה זֹּאת וְאָמַרְתָּ אֵלָיו. בְּחֹזֶק יָד הוֹצִיאָנוּ יְיָ מִמִּצְרַיִם מִבֵּית עֲבָדִים:

שֶׁאֵינוֹ יוֹדֵעַ לִשְׁאוֹל אַתְּ פְּתַח לוֹ. שֶׁנֶּאֱמַר וְהִגַּדְתָּ לְבִנְךָ בַּיּוֹם הַהוּא לֵאמֹר. בַּעֲבוּר זֶה עָשָׂה יְיָ לִי בְּצֵאתִי מִמִּצְרָיִם:

יָכוֹל מֵרֹאשׁ חֹדֶשׁ. תַּלְמוּד לוֹמַר בַּיּוֹם הַהוּא. אִי בַּיּוֹם הַהוּא יָכוֹל מִבְּעוֹד יוֹם. תַּלְמוּד לוֹמַר בַּעֲבוּר זֶה. בַּעֲבוּר זֶה לֹא אָמַרְתִּי אֶלָּא בְּשָׁעָה שֶׁיֵּשׁ מַצָּה וּמָרוֹר מֻנָּחִים לְפָנֶיךָ:

מִתְּחִלָּה עוֹבְדֵי עֲבוֹדָה זָרָה הָיוּ אֲבוֹתֵינוּ. וְעַכְשָׁו קֵרְבָנוּ הַמָּקוֹם לַעֲבוֹדָתוֹ. שֶׁנֶּאֱמַר וַיֹּאמֶר יְהוֹשֻׁעַ אֶל כָּל הָעָם. כֹּה אָמַר יְיָ אֱלֹהֵי יִשְׂרָאֵל. בְּעֵבֶר הַנָּהָר יָשְׁבוּ אֲבוֹתֵיכֶם מֵעוֹלָם. תֶּרַח אֲבִי אַבְרָהָם וַאֲבִי נָחוֹר. וַיַּעַבְדוּ אֱלֹהִים אֲחֵרִים. וָאֶקַּח אֶת אֲבִיכֶם אֶת אַבְרָהָם מֵעֵבֶר הַנָּהָר וָאוֹלֵךְ אוֹתוֹ בְּכָל אֶרֶץ כְּנָעַן. וָאַרְבֶּה אֶת זַרְעוֹ וָאֶתֶּן לוֹ אֶת יִצְחָק. וָאֶתֵּן לְיִצְחָק אֶת יַעֲקֹב וְאֶת עֵשָׂו. וָאֶתֵּן לְעֵשָׂו אֶת הַר שֵׂעִיר לָרֶשֶׁת אֹתוֹ וְיַעֲקֹב וּבָנָיו יָרְדוּ מִצְרָיִם:

THE FOUR SONS

The four sons are not simply four sons, or four children, but four types of people. At each Seder, we often find individuals who personify these four types. Here, as elsewhere in the Haggadah, the pedagogic goal that informs the Seder comes to the fore.

Note that we have translated the biblical verse in the wise son's question as ending with "upon us" rather than as in the Bible "upon you" to distinguish the wise from the wicked son, see Commentary, page 29. On the Four Sons and on Szyk's characterization of them, see Commentary, pages 28–32.

Blessed be the omnipresent God; blessed be he! Blessed is God who gave the Torah to his people Israel; blessed be he! The Torah discusses four types of sons: wise, wicked, simple, and one who does not know how to ask.

What does the wise one say? "What is the meaning of the statutes, laws, and ordinances that the Lord God has enjoined upon us?" (Deuteronomy 6:20). You should respond by informing him of all the laws relating to Passover, including [the ruling that] nothing should be eaten after the *Afikomen*.

What does the wicked one say? "What does this ritual mean to you?" (Exodus 12:26)—that is, "to *you*," but not to himself, which indicates that he excludes himself from the community and denies God. To him, you should respond caustically, saying, "This is because of what the Lord did for *me*, when *I* went out of Egypt" (Exodus 13:8), meaning: "for *me*," but not for "*him*"; that is, had he been there then, he would not have been liberated.

What does the simple one say? "What is this all about?" To him, you say, "It was with a mighty hand that the Lord brought us out of Egypt, out of the house of bondage" (Exodus 13:14).

And, as to the one who does not know how to ask, *you* should initiate the discussion with him. As it is written, "And you shall explain to your son on that day saying, 'This is because of what the Lord did for me when I went out of Egypt'" (Exodus 13:8).

After a short legal discussion (not translated here, but see Commentary, pages 25–27) the Haggadah presents the second Talmudic interpretation of "from shame to praise" by reminding us of the spiritual "degradation" of our idolatrous ancestors who preceded Abraham, and of how Abraham entered into an everlasting covenant with God that liberated us from idolatry.

Originally, our ancestors worshipped idols. But now, the omnipresent God has called us to his worship. As it is written, "Joshua said to all the people, 'So said the Lord, the God of Israel: In olden times your ancestors—Teraḥ, the father of Abraham, and Naḥor—lived beyond the [Euphrates] River, and they worshipped other gods. But I took your ancestor, Abraham, from beyond the river, and I led him through the entire land of Canaan, and multiplied his offspring. I gave him Isaac, and to Isaac I gave Jacob and Esau. To Esau, I gave the hill country of Mount Seir as his possession, while Jacob and his children went down to Egypt'" (Joshua 24:2–4).

שׁוֹמֵר הַבְטָחָתוֹ לְיִשְׂרָאֵל. בָּרוּךְ הוּא. שֶׁהַקָּדוֹשׁ בָּרוּךְ הוּא
חִשַּׁב אֶת הַקֵּץ. לַעֲשׂוֹת כְּמָה שֶׁאָמַר לְאַבְרָהָם אָבִינוּ בִּבְרִית
בֵּין הַבְּתָרִים שֶׁנֶּאֱמַר וַיֹּאמֶר לְאַבְרָם. יָדֹעַ תֵּדַע כִּי גֵר יִהְיֶה זַרְעֲךָ בְּאֶרֶץ לֹא
לָהֶם וַעֲבָדוּם וְעִנּוּ אֹתָם אַרְבַּע מֵאוֹת שָׁנָה: וְגַם אֶת הַגּוֹי אֲשֶׁר יַעֲבֹדוּ דָּן אָנֹכִי
וְאַחֲרֵי כֵן יֵצְאוּ בִּרְכֻשׁ גָּדוֹל:

מכסין את המצות ומגביהין את הכוס

הִיא שֶׁעָמְדָה לַאֲבוֹתֵינוּ
וְלָנוּ. שֶׁלֹּא אֶחָד בִּלְבַד
עָמַד עָלֵינוּ לְכַלּוֹתֵנוּ אֶלָּא
שֶׁבְּכָל דּוֹר וָדוֹר עוֹמְדִים
עָלֵינוּ לְכַלּוֹתֵנוּ. וְהַקָּדוֹשׁ
בָּרוּךְ הוּא מַצִּילֵנוּ מִיָּדָם:

ויניח הכוס ויגלה המצות

וְלָמַד מַה בִּקֵּשׁ לָבָן הָאֲרַ—מִי
לַעֲשׂוֹת לְיַעֲקֹב אָבִינוּ. שֶׁפַּרְעֹה
לֹא גָזַר אֶלָּא עַל הַזְּכָרִים וְלָבָן בִּקֵּשׁ לַעֲקוֹר
אֶת הַכֹּל שֶׁנֶּאֱמַר אֲרַמִּי אֹבֵד אָבִי וַיֵּרֶד
מִצְרַיְמָה וַיָּגָר שָׁם בִּמְתֵי מְעָט וַיְהִי שָׁם לְגוֹי
גָּדוֹל עָצוּם וָרָב: וַיֵּרֶד מִצְרַיְמָה. אָנוּס עַל פִּי
הַדִּבּוּר. וַיָּגָר שָׁם. מְלַמֵּד שֶׁלֹּא יָרַד יַעֲקֹב אָבִינוּ
לְהִשְׁתַּקֵּעַ בְּמִצְרַיִם אֶלָּא לָגוּר שָׁם שֶׁנֶּאֱמַר
וַיֹּאמְרוּ אֶל פַּרְעֹה. לָגוּר בָּאָרֶץ בָּאנוּ כִּי אֵין
מִרְעֶה לַצֹּאן אֲשֶׁר לַעֲבָדֶיךָ כִּי כָבֵד הָרָעָב בְּאֶרֶץ
כְּנָעַן וְעַתָּה יֵשְׁבוּ נָא עֲבָדֶיךָ בְּאֶרֶץ גֹּשֶׁן:

Blessed be he who keeps his promise to the people of Israel; blessed be he! For the Blessed Holy One determined the end [of our bondage] in fulfillment of what he promised Abraham, our ancestor, at the "Covenant between the Pieces" (see Genesis 15). As it is written, "And God said to Abraham, 'Know well that your offspring will be strangers in a land not their own, and there they will be enslaved and oppressed for four hundred years; but, I shall execute justice upon the nation they will serve, and after that they will go forth with great wealth'" (Genesis 15:13–14).

Both the preceding and following paragraphs summarize much of the experience of the Jewish people throughout their long history, seeing the movement from oppression to redemption as a motif running throughout Jewish history. For more on these themes, see Commentary, pages 33–36.

The matzot *are covered, and the wine cup is raised as the following is recited or sung, but no wine is drunk at this point.*

It is this [promise] that has stood by our forebears and us! For not just one [enemy] has stood against us to annihilate us, but in each and every generation they stand against us to annihilate us. Yet, the Blessed Holy One continues to deliver us from their hands.

V'hee sheh-ahm-dah lah-ah-voh-tei-noo v'lah-noo. Sheh-loh eḥad beel-vahd ah-mahd ah-lei-noo l'khah-loh-tei-noo, eh-lah sheh-b'khowl dohr vah-dohr, ohm-deem ah-lei-noo l'khah-loh-tei-noo. V'ha-kadosh barukh hoo matz-ee-lei-noo mee-yah-dahm.

This third rabbinic version of the "degradation to praise" narrative relates to the oppression of Jacob, also called "Israel," by his father-in-law, Laban. The story of oppression and redemption is seen as beginning earlier in Israelite history than the story of Passover. Laban is portrayed as even a greater oppressor than Pharaoh, for Pharaoh only wanted to murder all the firstborn sons of Israel while Laban wanted to annihilate the entire people of Israel, like many who would come after him.

Go forth and learn what Laban the Aramean desired to do to our ancestor Jacob. Whereas Pharaoh issued a decree [to murder] all [Hebrew] males, Laban aimed at destroying everyone. As it is written, "My ancestor was oppressed by an Aramean. He [Jacob] went down to Egypt with meager numbers and he sojourned there, but there he became a great and populous nation" (Deuteronomy 26:5).

מְתֵי מְעָט. כְּמָה שֶׁנֶּאֱמַר בְּשִׁבְעִים נֶפֶשׁ יָרְדוּ
אֲבוֹתֶיךָ מִצְרָיְמָה וְעַתָּה שָׂמְךָ יְיָ אֱלֹהֶיךָ כְּכוֹכְבֵי
הַשָּׁמַיִם לָרֹב: וַיְהִי שָׁם לְגוֹי. מְלַמֵּד שֶׁהָיוּ יִשְׂרָאֵל
מְצֻיָּנִים שָׁם: גָּדוֹל עָצוּם. כְּמָה שֶׁנֶּאֱמַר וּבְנֵי
יִשְׂרָאֵל פָּרוּ וַיִּשְׁרְצוּ וַיִּרְבּוּ וַיַּעַצְמוּ בִּמְאֹד מְאֹד
וַתִּמָּלֵא הָאָרֶץ אֹתָם:

וָרָב. כְּמָה שֶׁנֶּאֱמַר רְבָבָה כְּצֶמַח הַשָּׂדֶה
נְתַתִּיךְ וַתִּרְבִּי וַתִּגְדְּלִי וַתָּבֹאִי בַּעֲדִי
עֲדָיִים שָׁדַיִם נָכֹנוּ וּשְׂעָרֵךְ צִמֵּחַ וְאַתְּ עֵרֹם
וְעֶרְיָה: וָאֶעֱבֹר עָלַיִךְ וָאֶרְאֵךְ מִתְבּוֹסֶסֶת
בְּדָמָיִךְ וָאֹמַר לָךְ בְּדָמַיִךְ חֲיִי וָאֹמַר לָךְ בְּדָמַיִךְ
חֲיִי:

וַיָּרֵעוּ אֹתָנוּ הַמִּצְרִים וַיְעַנּוּנוּ וַיִּתְּנוּ עָלֵינוּ עֲבֹדָה קָשָׁה: וַיָּרֵעוּ אֹתָנוּ
הַמִּצְרִים כְּמָה שֶׁנֶּאֱמַר הָבָה נִתְחַכְּמָה לוֹ פֶּן יִרְבֶּה וְהָיָה כִּי
תִקְרֶאנָה מִלְחָמָה וְנוֹסַף גַּם הוּא עַל שֹׂנְאֵינוּ וְנִלְחַם בָּנוּ וְעָלָה מִן הָאָרֶץ:

וַיְעַנּוּנוּ. כְּמָה שֶׁנֶּאֱמַר וַיָּשִׂימוּ עָלָיו שָׂרֵי מִסִּים לְמַעַן עַנֹּתוֹ בְּסִבְלֹתָם
וַיִּבֶן עָרֵי מִסְכְּנוֹת לְפַרְעֹה אֶת פִּתֹם וְאֶת רַעַמְסֵס: וַיִּתְּנוּ עָלֵינוּ
עֲבֹדָה קָשָׁה. כְּמָה שֶׁנֶּאֱמַר וַיַּעֲבִדוּ מִצְרַיִם אֶת בְּנֵי יִשְׂרָאֵל בְּפָרֶךְ:

וַנִּצְעַק אֶל יְיָ אֱלֹהֵי אֲבֹתֵינוּ. וַיִּשְׁמַע יְיָ אֶת קֹלֵנוּ וַיַּרְא אֶת עָנְיֵנוּ וְאֶת
עֲמָלֵנוּ וְאֶת לַחֲצֵנוּ:

וַנִּצְעַק אֶל יְיָ אֱלֹהֵי אֲבֹתֵינוּ. כְּמָה
שֶׁנֶּאֱמַר וַיְהִי בַיָּמִים הָרַבִּים
הָהֵם וַיָּמָת מֶלֶךְ מִצְרַיִם וַיֵּאָנְחוּ
בְנֵי יִשְׂרָאֵל מִן הָעֲבֹדָה וַיִּזְעָקוּ
וַתַּעַל שַׁוְעָתָם אֶל הָאֱלֹהִים

Having cited Deuteronomy 26:5 in the last paragraph, the Haggadah continues with a section that offers rabbinic interpretations of the next immediate verses, Deuteronomy 26:6–8, which leads us directly into the presentation of the Ten Plagues. Excerpts of these rabbinic texts now follow.

Among other things, these texts provide a response to one of the most perplexing questions about how the Passover story is told in the Haggadah: why is there no mention of Moses and his role in the redemption from Egypt? On this question, see Commentary, pages 22–24.

NOTE: The Hebrew of the following translated excerpt can be found on the top of the next page. On this text, see Commentary, page 25.

["We cried to the Lord, the God of our ancestors, and the Lord heard our plea and saw our plight, our misery, and our oppression . . . " (Deuteronomy 26:7).] "The Lord heard our plea"—as the verse says, "God heard their cries, and God remembered his covenant with Abraham, Isaac, and Jacob" (Exodus 2:24). "And saw our plight"—referring to restraints on marital relations [so that male children would not be born and then murdered as per Pharaoh's decree], as it is written, "God looked upon the Israelites, and took notice of them." "Our plight"—referring to the plight of the [Israelite] male children. As it is written, "Every male child that is born, you must throw in the river Nile, but every female child may live" (Exodus 1:22). "Our oppression"—refers to severe persecution, as it is written, "Moreover I [God] have seen the harshness with which the Egyptians oppress them" (Exodus 3:9).

מִן הָעֲבֹדָה: וַיִּשְׁמַע יְיָ אֶת קֹלֵנוּ. כְּמָה שֶׁנֶּאֱמַר וַיִּשְׁמַע אֱלֹהִים אֶת נַאֲקָתָם וַיִּזְכֹּר
אֱלֹהִים אֶת בְּרִיתוֹ אֶת אַבְרָהָם אֶת יִצְחָק וְאֶת יַעֲקֹב: וַיַּרְא אֶת עָנְיֵנוּ. זוֹ פְּרִישׁוּת
דֶּרֶךְ אֶרֶץ. כְּמָה שֶׁנֶּאֱמַר וַיַּרְא אֱלֹהִים אֶת בְּנֵי יִשְׂרָאֵל וַיֵּדַע אֱלֹהִים: וְאֶת עֲמָלֵנוּ
אֵלּוּ הַבָּנִים. כְּמָה שֶׁנֶּאֱמַר כָּל הַבֵּן הַיִּלּוֹד הַיְאֹרָה תַּשְׁלִיכוּהוּ וְכָל הַבַּת תְּחַיּוּן:
וְאֶת לַחֲצֵנוּ. זוֹ הַדְּחַק. כְּמָה שֶׁנֶּאֱמַר וְגַם רָאִיתִי אֶת הַלַּחַץ אֲשֶׁר מִצְרַיִם לֹחֲצִים אֹתָם:

וַיּוֹצִאֵנוּ יְיָ מִמִּצְרַיִם בְּיָד חֲזָקָה וּבִזְרֹעַ נְטוּיָה וּבְמֹרָא גָּדֹל וּבְאֹתוֹת
וּבְמֹפְתִים:

וַיּוֹצִאֵנוּ יְיָ מִמִּצְרַיִם. לֹא עַל יְדֵי מַלְאָךְ וְלֹא עַל יְדֵי שָׂרָף וְלֹא עַל
יְדֵי שָׁלִיחַ. אֶלָּא הַקָּדוֹשׁ בָּרוּךְ הוּא בִּכְבוֹדוֹ וּבְעַצְמוֹ. שֶׁנֶּאֱמַר
וְעָבַרְתִּי בְאֶרֶץ מִצְרַיִם בַּלַּיְלָה הַזֶּה וְהִכֵּיתִי כָל בְּכוֹר בְּאֶרֶץ מִצְרַיִם מֵאָדָם וְעַד
בְּהֵמָה וּבְכָל אֱלֹהֵי מִצְרַיִם אֶעֱשֶׂה שְׁפָטִים אֲנִי יְיָ: וְעָבַרְתִּי בְאֶרֶץ מִצְרַיִם
בַּלַּיְלָה הַזֶּה. אֲנִי וְלֹא מַלְאָךְ. וְהִכֵּיתִי כָל בְּכוֹר בְּאֶרֶץ מִצְרַיִם. אֲנִי וְלֹא שָׂרָף
וּבְכָל אֱלֹהֵי מִצְרַיִם אֶעֱשֶׂה שְׁפָטִים אֲנִי יְיָ. אֲנִי הוּא וְלֹא הַשָּׁלִיחַ. אֲנִי יְיָ. אֲנִי הוּא
וְלֹא אַחֵר:

בְּיָד חֲזָקָה. זוֹ הַדֶּבֶר. כְּמָה שֶׁנֶּאֱמַר הִנֵּה יַד יְיָ הוֹיָה בְּמִקְנְךָ אֲשֶׁר בַּשָּׂדֶה בַּסּוּסִים בַּחֲמֹרִים
בַּגְּמַלִּים בַּבָּקָר וּבַצֹּאן דֶּבֶר כָּבֵד מְאֹד: וּבִזְרֹעַ נְטוּיָה. זוֹ הַחֶרֶב. כְּמָה שֶׁנֶּאֱמַר וְחַרְבּוֹ שְׁלוּפָה
בְּיָדוֹ נְטוּיָה עַל יְרוּשָׁלַיִם. וּבְמֹרָא גָּדֹל. זוֹ גִּלּוּי שְׁכִינָה. כְּמָה שֶׁנֶּאֱמַר אוֹ הֲנִסָּה אֱלֹהִים
לָבוֹא לָקַחַת לוֹ גוֹי מִקֶּרֶב גּוֹי בְּמַסֹּת בְּאֹתֹת וּבְמוֹפְתִים וּבְמִלְחָמָה וּבְיָד חֲזָקָה וּבִזְרוֹעַ נְטוּיָה
וּבְמוֹרָאִים גְּדֹלִים. כְּכֹל אֲשֶׁר עָשָׂה לָכֶם יְיָ אֱלֹהֵיכֶם בְּמִצְרַיִם לְעֵינֶיךָ: וּבְאֹתֹת. זֶה הַמַּטֶּה. כְּמָה שֶׁנֶּאֱמַר וְאֶת הַמַּטֶּה הַזֶּה
תִּקַּח בְּיָדֶךָ אֲשֶׁר תַּעֲשֶׂה בּוֹ אֶת הָאֹתֹת: וּבְמֹפְתִים. זֶה הַדָּם. כְּמָה שֶׁנֶּאֱמַר וְנָתַתִּי מוֹפְתִים בַּשָּׁמַיִם וּבָאָרֶץ

דָּם וָאֵשׁ וְתִמְרוֹת עָשָׁן.

אַחֵר. בְּיָד חֲזָקָה שְׁתַּיִם. וּבִזְרֹעַ נְטוּיָה שְׁתַּיִם. וּבְמֹרָא גָּדֹל שְׁתַּיִם. וּבְאֹתֹת שְׁתַּיִם. וּבְמֹפְתִים שְׁתַּיִם: אֵלּוּ
עֶשֶׂר מַכּוֹת שֶׁהֵבִיא הַקָּדוֹשׁ בָּרוּךְ הוּא עַל הַמִּצְרִים בְּמִצְרַיִם. וְאֵלּוּ הֵן:

דָּם. צְפַרְדֵּעַ. כִּנִּים. עָרוֹב. דֶּבֶר.
שְׁחִין. בָּרָד. אַרְבֶּה. חֹשֶׁךְ. מַכַּת בְּכוֹרוֹת.

Discussion now continues with the next verse in the sequence, Deuteronomy 26:8:

"The Lord brought us out of Egypt with a mighty hand, an outstretched arm, great power, and with miracles and portents."

"The Lord brought us out of Egypt"—not by the agency of an angel, a *seraph,* or a human being, but by the Blessed Holy One, by himself and in his glory. As it is written, "I shall pass through Egypt on that night to strike down every firstborn [Egyptian] in the Land of Egypt, human and animal; and, I shall mete out punishments upon all the gods of Egypt, I the Lord" (Exodus 12:12). "I shall pass through Egypt"—meaning: I, the Lord. "To strike down every firstborn in the Land of Egypt"—meaning: I, and not a seraph. "And I shall mete out punishments upon all the gods of Egypt"—meaning: I, and not a[n] [human] agent. "I the Lord"—meaning: I am he, and no other.

"With a mighty hand"—referring to the pestilence [brought by God upon the Egyptians,] as it is written, "Behold the hand of the Lord will strike your livestock in the fields—horses, donkeys, camels, cattle, and sheep—with a very severe pestilence" (Exodus 9:3). "An outstretched arm"—referring to the sword. As it is written, "with a drawn sword in his [that is, an angel's] hand directed against Jerusalem" (1 Chronicles 21:16). "Great power"—refers to the revelation of the *Shekhinah,* the Divine Presence. As it is written, "Has any divine being ventured to go and take for itself one nation from the midst of another nation by prodigious acts, signs and wonders, and by war, and with a mighty hand and an outstretched arm and awesome power in everything, as the Lord your God did for you in Egypt before your very eyes?" (Deuteronomy 4:34). "Miracles"—refers to [Moses'] rod, as it is written, "Take this rod in your hand, with which you shall perform miraculous signs" (Exodus 4:17). "Portents"—refers to blood. As it is written, "I shall set portents in the sky and on the earth; blood, fire, pillars of smoke" [depicted to the right] (Joel 3:3).

Yet, there is a further explanation; namely, that each of these five phrases— "with a mighty hand," "an outstretched arm," "great power," "miracles," and "portents"—denotes two plagues which together constitute the ten plagues that the Blessed Holy One brought upon the Egyptians in Egypt [that is, five phrases times two plagues, equals ten plagues]. And these are they:

BLOOD   FROGS   LICE   WILD BEASTS   CATTLE DISEASE   BOILS HAIL   LOCUSTS   DARKNESS   SMITING OF THE FIRSTBORN

שְׁחִין   דָּם

בָּרָד   צְפַרְדֵּעַ

עָרֹב   כִּנִּים

חֹשֶׁךְ   אַרְבֶּה

מַכַּת בְּכוֹרוֹת   דֶּבֶר

THE TEN PLAGUES

On the facing page is Szyk's depiction of the Ten Plagues that God brought in Egypt upon the Egyptians. The Talmudic rabbis debated the number of plagues that God brought in Egypt. They also debated the number of plagues God brought against the Egyptians at the Sea of Reeds (the Red Sea). These debates are found in Hebrew on the next page. Though left untranslated here, those texts are discussed in Commentary, pages 39–40. Rabbi Yehudah composed a mnemonic in Hebrew to help people remember the names of the Ten Plagues, consisting of the first Hebrew letters of the names of each of the plagues, which he then divided into three "words." Although it appears on the top of the next page, this mnemonic is cited below.

Though absent from Szyk's instructions for conducting the Seder, it is common practice for each Seder participant to recite the names of each of the plagues while spilling out some wine onto a dish to represent each of the plagues. Most people follow the custom of spilling out wine for each of the Ten Plagues, while others spill out thirteen times, and still others sixteen times. The wine spilled out is later discarded. The origins and explanations of these practices are discussed in Commentary, pages 39–40.

The Ten Plagues are:

Dahm—**Blood**
Tz'fahr-dei-ah—**Frogs**
Kee-neem—**Lice**
Ahr-ohv—**Wild Beasts**
Deh-vehr—**Cattle Disease**
Sh'ḥeen—**Boils**
Bah-rahd—**Hail**
Ahr-beh—**Locusts**
Ḥoh-shekh—**Darkness**
Mah-kaht B'khoh-roht—**Smiting of the Firstborn**

Rabbi Yehudah composed a [ten-letter] Hebrew mnemonic [based on the names of the plagues]:

דְּצַ"ךְ עֲדַ"שׁ בְּאַחַ"ב

D'TZ-aKH Ah-Dah-SH B'A-Ḥa-B

דְּצַ"ךְ עַדַ"שׁ בְּאַחַ"ב

רַבִּי יוֹסֵי הַגְּלִילִי אוֹמֵר. מִנַּיִן אַתָּה אוֹמֵר שֶׁלָּקוּ הַמִּצְרִים בְּמִצְרַיִם עֶשֶׂר מַכּוֹת וְעַל הַיָּם לָקוּ חֲמִשִּׁים מַכּוֹת. בְּמִצְרַיִם מָה הוּא אוֹמֵר. וַיֹּאמְרוּ הַחַרְטֻמִּים אֶל פַּרְעֹה אֶצְבַּע אֱלֹהִים הוּא. וְעַל הַיָּם מָה הוּא אוֹמֵר. וַיַּרְא יִשְׂרָאֵל אֶת הַיָּד הַגְּדוֹלָה אֲשֶׁר עָשָׂה יְיָ בְּמִצְרַיִם. וַיִּירְאוּ הָעָם אֶת יְיָ וַיַּאֲמִינוּ בַּייָ וּבְמֹשֶׁה עַבְדּוֹ: כַּמָּה לָקוּ בָאֶצְבַּע. עֶשֶׂר מַכּוֹת. אֱמוֹר מֵעַתָּה בְּמִצְרַיִם לָקוּ עֶשֶׂר מַכּוֹת וְעַל הַיָּם לָקוּ חֲמִשִּׁים מַכּוֹת:

רַבִּי אֱלִיעֶזֶר אוֹמֵר. מִנַּיִן שֶׁכָּל מַכָּה וּמַכָּה שֶׁהֵבִיא הַקָּדוֹשׁ בָּרוּךְ הוּא עַל הַמִּצְרִים בְּמִצְרַיִם הָיְתָה שֶׁל אַרְבַּע מַכּוֹת. שֶׁנֶּאֱמַר יְשַׁלַּח בָּם חֲרוֹן אַפּוֹ עֶבְרָה וָזַעַם וְצָרָה מִשְׁלַחַת מַלְאֲכֵי רָעִים. עֶבְרָה אַחַת. וָזַעַם שְׁתַּיִם. וְצָרָה שָׁלֹשׁ. מִשְׁלַחַת מַלְאֲכֵי רָעִים אַרְבַּע. אֱמוֹר מֵעַתָּה בְּמִצְרַיִם לָקוּ אַרְבָּעִים מַכּוֹת וְעַל הַיָּם לָקוּ מָאתַיִם מַכּוֹת:

רַבִּי עֲקִיבָא אוֹמֵר. מִנַּיִן שֶׁכָּל מַכָּה וּמַכָּה שֶׁהֵבִיא הַקָּדוֹשׁ בָּרוּךְ הוּא עַל הַמִּצְרִים בְּמִצְרַיִם הָיְתָה שֶׁל חָמֵשׁ מַכּוֹת. שֶׁנֶּאֱמַר יְשַׁלַּח בָּם חֲרוֹן אַפּוֹ עֶבְרָה וָזַעַם וְצָרָה מִשְׁלַחַת מַלְאֲכֵי רָעִים. חֲרוֹן אַפּוֹ אַחַת. עֶבְרָה שְׁתַּיִם. וָזַעַם שָׁלֹשׁ. וְצָרָה אַרְבַּע. מִשְׁלַחַת מַלְאֲכֵי רָעִים חָמֵשׁ. אֱמוֹר מֵעַתָּה בְּמִצְרַיִם לָקוּ חֲמִשִּׁים מַכּוֹת וְעַל הַיָּם לָקוּ חֲמִשִּׁים וּמָאתַיִם מַכּוֹת:

כַּמָּה מַעֲלוֹת טוֹבוֹת לַמָּקוֹם עָלֵינוּ

וַיִּקַּח דָּוִד אֶת רֹאשׁ הַפְּלִשְׁתִּי

אִלּוּ הוֹצִיאָנוּ מִמִּצְרַיִם וְלֹא עָשָׂה בָהֶם שְׁפָטִים דַּיֵּנוּ:

אִלּוּ עָשָׂה בָהֶם שְׁפָטִים וְלֹא עָשָׂה בֵאלֹהֵיהֶם דַּיֵּנוּ:

אִלּוּ עָשָׂה בֵאלֹהֵיהֶם וְלֹא הָרַג אֶת בְּכוֹרֵיהֶם דַּיֵּנוּ:

אִלּוּ הָרַג אֶת בְּכוֹרֵיהֶם וְלֹא נָתַן לָנוּ אֶת מָמוֹנָם דַּיֵּנוּ:

אִלּוּ נָתַן לָנוּ אֶת מָמוֹנָם וְלֹא קָרַע לָנוּ אֶת הַיָּם דַּיֵּנוּ:

אִלּוּ קָרַע לָנוּ אֶת הַיָּם וְלֹא הֶעֱבִירָנוּ בְתוֹכוֹ בֶּחָרָבָה דַּיֵּנוּ:

אִלּוּ הֶעֱבִירָנוּ בְתוֹכוֹ בֶּחָרָבָה וְלֹא שִׁקַּע צָרֵינוּ בְּתוֹכוֹ דַּיֵּנוּ:

אִלּוּ שִׁקַּע צָרֵינוּ בְּתוֹכוֹ וְלֹא סִפֵּק צָרְכֵּנוּ בַּמִּדְבָּר אַרְבָּעִים שָׁנָה דַּיֵּנוּ:

אִלּוּ סִפֵּק צָרְכֵּנוּ בַּמִּדְבָּר אַרְבָּעִים שָׁנָה וְלֹא הֶאֱכִילָנוּ אֶת הַמָּן דַּיֵּנוּ:

אִלּוּ הֶאֱכִילָנוּ אֶת הַמָּן וְלֹא נָתַן לָנוּ אֶת הַשַּׁבָּת דַּיֵּנוּ:

אִלּוּ נָתַן לָנוּ אֶת הַשַּׁבָּת וְלֹא קֵרְבָנוּ לִפְנֵי הַר סִינַי דַּיֵּנוּ:

אִלּוּ קֵרְבָנוּ לִפְנֵי הַר סִינַי וְלֹא נָתַן לָנוּ אֶת הַתּוֹרָה דַּיֵּנוּ:

אִלּוּ נָתַן לָנוּ אֶת הַתּוֹרָה וְלֹא הִכְנִיסָנוּ לְאֶרֶץ יִשְׂרָאֵל דַּיֵּנוּ:

אִלּוּ הִכְנִיסָנוּ לְאֶרֶץ יִשְׂרָאֵל וְלֹא בָנָה לָנוּ אֶת בֵּית הַבְּחִירָה דַּיֵּנוּ:

"DAYENU"

On the lower part of the facing Hebrew page, we have the signature song of the Seder, "Dayenu," a song that echoes in the ears of Seder participants long after Passover. The author is unknown. Alluding to a variety of biblical, Talmudic, and midrashic texts, "Dayenu" seems to have been composed in the immediately post-Talmudic era, perhaps around the seventh or eighth century. "Dayenu" has fifteen stanzas, paralleling the fifteen parts of the Seder.

Usually someone sings each of the stanzas with all participants joining in to sing the refrain:

Dy-dayenu, dy-dayenu, dy-dayenu, dayenu, dayenu, dayenu. Dy-dayenu, dy-dayenu, dy-dayenu, dayenu dayenu.

*D*AYENU!—"It Would Have Sufficed for Us!"
How many acts of escalating kindness has the omnipresent God performed on our behalf!
Had he brought us out of Egypt, but not also wrought judgment upon them

    [that is, upon the Egyptians]   *—Dayenu!*

Had he wrought judgment upon them, but not also upon their gods   *—Dayenu!*

Had he wrought judgment upon their gods, but not also slain their firstborn   *—Dayenu!*

Had he slain their firstborn, but not also given us their wealth   *—Dayenu!*

Had he given us their wealth, but not also split the sea for us   *—Dayenu!*

Had he split the sea for us, and not also brought us through the sea dry-shod   *—Dayenu!*

Had he brought us through it dry-shod, but not also drowned our oppressors in it   *—Dayenu!*

Had he drowned our oppressors in it, but not also fulfilled our needs in the desert

    for forty years   *—Dayenu!*

Had he fulfilled our needs in the desert for forty years, but not also fed us

    with manna   *—Dayenu!*

Had he fed us with manna, but not also given us the Sabbath   *—Dayenu!*

Had he given us the Sabbath, but not also brought us to the foot of Mount Sinai   *—Dayenu!*

Had he brought us to the foot of Mount Sinai, but not also given us the Torah   *—Dayenu!*

Had he given us the Torah, but not also admitted us into the Land of Israel   *—Dayenu!*

Had he admitted us into the Land of Israel, but not also built for us the Holy Temple   *—Dayenu!*

NOTE: Usually transliterated as *dayenu*, this word is pronounced *dy-ay-noo*.

ל אַחַת כַּמָּה וְכַמָּה טוֹבָה כְּפוּלָה וּמְכֻפֶּלֶת לַמָּקוֹם
עָלֵינוּ. שֶׁהוֹצִיאָנוּ מִמִּצְרַיִם. וְעָשָׂה בָהֶם שְׁפָטִים. וְעָשָׂה
בֵאלֹהֵיהֶם. וְהָרַג אֶת בְּכוֹרֵיהֶם. וְנָתַן לָנוּ אֶת מָמוֹנָם.
וְקָרַע לָנוּ אֶת הַיָּם. וְהֶעֱבִירָנוּ בְתוֹכוֹ בֶּחָרָבָה. וְשִׁקַּע
צָרֵינוּ בְּתוֹכוֹ. וְסִפֵּק צָרְכֵּנוּ בַּמִּדְבָּר אַרְבָּעִים שָׁנָה
וְהֶאֱכִילָנוּ אֶת הַמָּן. וְנָתַן לָנוּ אֶת הַשַּׁבָּת. וְקֵרְבָנוּ לִפְנֵי
הַר סִינַי. וְנָתַן לָנוּ אֶת הַתּוֹרָה. וְהִכְנִיסָנוּ לְאֶרֶץ יִשְׂרָאֵל
וּבָנָה לָנוּ אֶת בֵּית הַבְּחִירָה. לְכַפֵּר עַל כָּל עֲוֹנוֹתֵינוּ:

גַּמְלִיאֵל הָיָה אוֹמֵר. כָּל שֶׁלֹּא אָמַר שְׁלֹשָׁה דְבָרִים אֵלּוּ בַּפֶּסַח לֹא
יָצָא יְדֵי חוֹבָתוֹ. וְאֵלּוּ הֵן.

פֶּסַח מַצָּה וּמָרוֹר

שֶׁהָיוּ אֲבוֹתֵינוּ אוֹכְלִים בִּזְמַן שֶׁבֵּית הַמִּקְדָּשׁ קַיָּם
עַל שׁוּם מָה. עַל שׁוּם שֶׁפָּסַח הַקָּדוֹשׁ בָּרוּךְ הוּא עַל בָּתֵּי
אֲבוֹתֵינוּ בְּמִצְרַיִם. שֶׁנֶּאֱמַר וַאֲמַרְתֶּם זֶבַח פֶּסַח הוּא
לַיי. אֲשֶׁר פָּסַח עַל בָּתֵּי בְנֵי יִשְׂרָאֵל בְּמִצְרַיִם בְּנָגְפּוֹ
אֶת מִצְרַיִם וְאֶת בָּתֵּינוּ הִצִּיל. וַיִּקֹּד הָעָם וַיִּשְׁתַּחֲווּ:

The second part of "Dayenu," left untranslated here, is a summary of the song and an expression of gratitude to God for God's many bounties. In this version, however, the Temple is described as a vehicle for atoning for our sins. In this view, through atonement and repentance, we make ourselves worthy of redemption and thereby play an active role in the redemptive process.

Rabban Gamliel used to say, "Anyone who does not make mention of these three things on Passover, has not fulfilled his obligations." These [three] are:

The Paschal Lamb—*Pesaḥ*
Unleavened Bread—*Matzah*
Bitter Herbs—*Mah-rohr*

In the Mishnah, from which Rabban Gamliel's statement derives, he explains why we make mention of the Paschal lamb, the *matzah*, and the bitter herbs at the Seder. According to Rabban Gamliel, the *Pesaḥ* (literally, the Passover) or Paschal lamb, reminds us that "God passed over the homes of our ancestors in Egypt" during the tenth plague—the killing of the firstborn sons of Egypt (*Mishnah, Pesaḥim* 10:5). See Commentary, pages 15–17.

Unlike the matzah *and bitter herbs, the shank bone, symbolizing the Paschal sacrifice is neither held, eaten, nor even pointed to.*

Pesaḥ—the Paschal lamb that our ancestors ate when the Temple was standing—why was it eaten? It was because the Blessed Holy One passed over the houses of our ancestors in Egypt. ["When your children ask you, 'What do you mean by this rite?'"] you shall respond as it is written, "It is the Passover sacrifice to the Lord because he passed over the houses of the Israelites in Egypt when he smote the Egyptians, but saved our houses; and, the people bowed in homage" (Exodus 12:27).

מַרְאֶה הַמַּצָּה לַמְסוּבִּין וְאוֹמֵר:

זוֹ שֶׁאָנוּ אוֹכְלִין עַל שׁוּם מַה. עַל שׁוּם שֶׁלֹּא הִסְפִּיק בְּצֵקָם שֶׁל אֲבוֹתֵינוּ לְהַחֲמִיץ. עַד שֶׁנִּגְלָה עֲלֵיהֶם מֶלֶךְ מַלְכֵי הַמְּלָכִים הַקָּדוֹשׁ בָּרוּךְ הוּא וּגְאָלָם. שֶׁנֶּאֱמַר וַיֹּאפוּ אֶת הַבָּצֵק אֲשֶׁר הוֹצִיאוּ מִמִּצְרַיִם עֻגֹת מַצּוֹת כִּי לֹא חָמֵץ כִּי גֹרְשׁוּ מִמִּצְרַיִם. וְלֹא יָכְלוּ לְהִתְמַהְמֵהַּ. וְגַם צֵדָה לֹא עָשׂוּ לָהֶם:

מַרְאֶה הַמָּרוֹר לַמְסוּבִּין וְאוֹמֵר:

זֶה שֶׁאָנוּ אוֹכְלִין עַל שׁוּם מַה. עַל שׁוּם שֶׁמֵּרְרוּ הַמִּצְרִים אֶת חַיֵּי אֲבוֹתֵינוּ בְּמִצְרַיִם. שֶׁנֶּאֱמַר וַיְמָרְרוּ אֶת חַיֵּיהֶם בַּעֲבֹדָה קָשָׁה בְּחֹמֶר וּבִלְבֵנִים וּבְכָל עֲבֹדָה בַּשָּׂדֶה. אֵת כָּל עֲבֹדָתָם אֲשֶׁר עָבְדוּ בָהֶם בְּפָרֶךְ:

כָּל דּוֹר וָדוֹר חַיָּב אָדָם לִרְאוֹת אֶת עַצְמוֹ כְּאִלּוּ הוּא יָצָא מִמִּצְרַיִם. שֶׁנֶּאֱמַר וְהִגַּדְתָּ לְבִנְךָ בַּיּוֹם הַהוּא לֵאמֹר. בַּעֲבוּר זֶה עָשָׂה יְיָ לִי בְּצֵאתִי מִמִּצְרָיִם. לֹא אֶת אֲבוֹתֵינוּ בִּלְבַד גָּאַל הַקָּדוֹשׁ בָּרוּךְ הוּא. אֶלָּא אַף אוֹתָנוּ גָּאַל עִמָּהֶם. שֶׁנֶּאֱמַר וְאוֹתָנוּ הוֹצִיא מִשָּׁם לְמַעַן הָבִיא אֹתָנוּ לָתֶת לָנוּ אֶת הָאָרֶץ אֲשֶׁר נִשְׁבַּע לַאֲבֹתֵינוּ:

According to Rabban Gamliel, *matzah* is mentioned to remind us that God "redeemed our ancestors from Egypt."

The matzah *is held up and shown to everyone, and one of the participants in the Seder says:*

> This *matzah*: Why do we eat it? [To remind us] that even before the dough of our ancestors had time to rise, the supreme King of Kings, the Blessed Holy One, revealed himself to them, and redeemed them, as it is written, "They baked unleavened cakes of the dough that they had brought out of Egypt, for it was not leavened, since they had been driven out of Egypt and could not delay; nor had they prepared any provisions for themselves" (Exodus 12:39).

According to Rabban Gamliel, bitter herbs are eaten to remind us that "the Egyptians embittered the lives of our ancestors in Egypt."

The bitter herbs are held up and shown to everyone, and one of the participants says:

> These bitter herbs: Why do we eat them? [To remind us] that the Egyptians embittered the lives of our ancestors in Egypt, as it is written, "They [that is, the Egyptians] embittered their lives with harsh labor, with mortar and bricks, and with every manner of drudgery in the field, and they worked them ruthlessly in all their labor" (Exodus 1:14).

In the following single statement, also based upon the words of Rabban Gamliel, we have a summary of the purpose of the Seder: to remember the Exodus as a formative event in Jewish experience, to tell the story of Passover, to convey the memory of that event to members of the next generation, and to internalize the memory of that event, not only as a collective experience in the distant past, but also as a personal, individual experience in the present. Accordingly, each individual should seek to be liberated on Passover from his or her own personal "Egypt." On Passover and individual redemption, see Commentary, pages 38–39.

> In each generation, each individual Jew is obliged to regard himself or herself as if he or she had personally gone out of Egypt. As it is written, "You should tell your child on that day, saying: 'This is because of what the Lord did for *me* when *I* went out of Egypt'" (Exodus 13:8). For it was not our ancestors alone who the Holy One did redeem, but he also redeemed us with them, as it is written, "He brought *us* out of there, so that he might bring us to the land, and give us the land that he promised to our ancestors" (Deuteronomy 6:23).

מכסין המצות ומגביהין הכוס ואומרין בקול רם ‪:‬

פִּיכָךְ אֲנַחְנוּ חַיָּבִים לְהוֹדוֹת
לְהַלֵּל לְשַׁבֵּחַ לְפָאֵר לְרוֹמֵם לְהַדֵּר
לְבָרֵךְ לְעַלֵּה וּלְקַלֵּס לְמִי שֶׁעָשָׂה
לַאֲבוֹתֵינוּ וְלָנוּ אֶת כָּל הַנִּסִּים הָאֵלּוּ
הוֹצִיאָנוּ מֵעַבְדוּת לְחֵרוּת‪.‬ מִיָּגוֹן לְשִׂמְחָה
וּמֵאֵבֶל לְיוֹם טוֹב‪.‬ וּמֵאֲפֵלָה לְאוֹר
גָּדוֹל‪.‬ וּמִשִּׁעְבּוּד לִגְאֻלָּה‪.‬ וְנֹאמַר
לְפָנָיו שִׁירָה חֲדָשָׁה

הַלְלוּיָהּ

Again here, the text recalls a statement by Rabban Gamliel (*Mishnah*, *Pesaḥim* 10:5). This serves as a transition between telling the story of Passover and reciting psalms and prayers in praise of God for God's having redeemed the Israelites from Egypt. This transition reflects the rabbinic directive, discussed above, that has the storyline of Passover move from "shame and degradation to praise."

The matzot *are covered, the cup is raised, and the following is recited, but we do not drink the wine.*

Therefore, we are obliged to thank, praise, laud, glorify, exalt, adore, bless, extol, and honor the One who performed all these miracles for our forebears and for us. He brought us out from slavery to freedom, from sorrow to joy, from mourning to festivity, from darkness to light, and from servitude to redemption. Let us therefore sing a new song in his presence. *Halleluyah*—Praise God!

הַלְלוּיָהּ וְלֹא שָׁתוּ בְּצִלּוֹ חֲלֻשׁ:

הַלְלוּ עַבְדֵי יְיָ הַלְלוּ אֶת שֵׁם יְיָ: יְהִי שֵׁם יְיָ מְבֹרָךְ מֵעַתָּה וְעַד עוֹלָם: מִמִּזְרַח שֶׁמֶשׁ עַד מְבוֹאוֹ מְהֻלָּל שֵׁם יְיָ: רָם עַל כָּל גּוֹיִם יְיָ עַל הַשָּׁמַיִם כְּבוֹדוֹ: מִי כַּיְיָ אֱלֹהֵינוּ הַמַּגְבִּיהִי לָשָׁבֶת: הַמַּשְׁפִּילִי לִרְאוֹת בַּשָּׁמַיִם וּבָאָרֶץ: מְקִימִי מֵעָפָר דָּל מֵאַשְׁפֹּת יָרִים אֶבְיוֹן: לְהוֹשִׁיבִי עִם נְדִיבִים עִם נְדִיבֵי עַמּוֹ: מוֹשִׁיבִי עֲקֶרֶת הַבַּיִת אֵם הַבָּנִים שְׂמֵחָה הַלְלוּיָהּ:

בְּצֵאת יִשְׂרָאֵל מִמִּצְרָיִם בֵּית יַעֲקֹב מֵעַם לֹעֵז: הָיְתָה יְהוּדָה לְקָדְשׁוֹ יִשְׂרָאֵל מַמְשְׁלוֹתָיו: הַיָּם רָאָה וַיָּנֹס הַיַּרְדֵּן יִסֹּב לְאָחוֹר: הֶהָרִים רָקְדוּ כְאֵילִים גְּבָעוֹת כִּבְנֵי צֹאן: מַה לְּךָ הַיָּם כִּי תָנוּס הַיַּרְדֵּן תִּסֹּב לְאָחוֹר: הֶהָרִים תִּרְקְדוּ כְאֵילִים גְּבָעוֹת כִּבְנֵי צֹאן: מִלִּפְנֵי אָדוֹן חוּלִי אָרֶץ מִלִּפְנֵי אֱלוֹהַּ יַעֲקֹב: הַהֹפְכִי הַצּוּר אֲגַם מָיִם חַלָּמִישׁ לְמַעְיְנוֹ מָיִם:

נוֹטֵל אֶת הַכּוֹס בְּיָדוֹ וְיֹאמַר זֶה.

אַתָּה יְיָ אֱלֹהֵינוּ מֶלֶךְ הָעוֹלָם אֲשֶׁר גְּאָלָנוּ וְגָאַל אֶת אֲבוֹתֵינוּ מִמִּצְרַיִם וְהִגִּיעָנוּ הַלַּיְלָה הַזֶּה לֶאֱכָל בּוֹ מַצָּה וּמָרוֹר: כֵּן יְיָ אֱלֹהֵינוּ וֵאלֹהֵי אֲבוֹתֵינוּ יַגִּיעֵנוּ לְמוֹעֲדִים וְלִרְגָלִים אֲחֵרִים הַבָּאִים לִקְרָאתֵנוּ לְשָׁלוֹם: שְׂמֵחִים בְּבִנְיַן עִירֶךָ וְשָׂשִׂים בַּעֲבוֹדָתֶךָ. וְנֹאכַל שָׁם מִן הַזְּבָחִים וּמִן הַפְּסָחִים (בְּמוֹצָאֵי שַׁבָּת אוֹמְרִים: מִן הַפְּסָחִים וּמִן הַזְּבָחִים) אֲשֶׁר יַגִּיעַ דָּמָם עַל קִיר מִזְבַּחֲךָ לְרָצוֹן. וְנוֹדֶה לְךָ שִׁיר חָדָשׁ עַל גְּאֻלָּתֵנוּ וְעַל פְּדוּת נַפְשֵׁנוּ: בָּרוּךְ אַתָּה יְיָ גָּאַל יִשְׂרָאֵל:

Two psalms that form part of liturgical section known as the *Halleil* are now recited, Psalms 113 and 114. Here we translate Psalm 114, which celebrates the Exodus from Egypt. Psalm 113, which offers generic praise of God for his mercies, is left untranslated.

To the text that follows, Szyk adds this caption: "In all of my sacred mountain, nothing vile or evil shall be done" (Isaiah 11:9, 65:25).

PSALM 114

When Israel left Egypt, the House of Jacob from a people of a foreign tongue, Judah became God's sanctuary, Israel became his dominion. The Sea [of Reeds] saw them and fled. The Jordan [River] flowed backward. The mountains skipped like rams; the hills [leaped] like sheep. What alarmed you, O sea, that you fled? [Why] Jordan, did you flow backward? [Why] did you mountains skip like rams, [and you] hills [leap] like sheep? Tremble, O earth, before the Master of the earth, before the God of Jacob. God turned the rock into a pool of water, the solid stone into a fountain.

What now follows is a long blessing that thanks God for the privilege of celebrating the Passover and expresses the hope for a complete redemption in the near future. It serves as a transition from the fifth section of the Seder—telling the story, *Maggid*—to the rest of the Seder.

Everyone raises their cup of wine and the following prayer is recited, though without drinking the wine:

Blessed are you, Lord our God, Sovereign of the Universe, who redeemed us and our ancestors from Egypt, and enabled us to reach this night [to fulfill the commandment] of eating *matzah* and *mah-rohr*, the bitter herbs. So, too, Lord our God, may you enable us to observe future festivals and holydays in peace, happy because of the rebuilding of your city [Jerusalem] and joyous in your sacred service. There [at the rebuilt Temple in Jerusalem], may we eat of the sacrifices and of the sacrificial Passover offerings (*on Saturday night, say instead: Passover offerings and sacrifices*), the blood of which will be sprinkled on the wall of your altar for your acceptance. Then, we shall thank you with a new song for our redemption and for our personal deliverance. Blessed are you, God, who has redeemed the people of Israel.

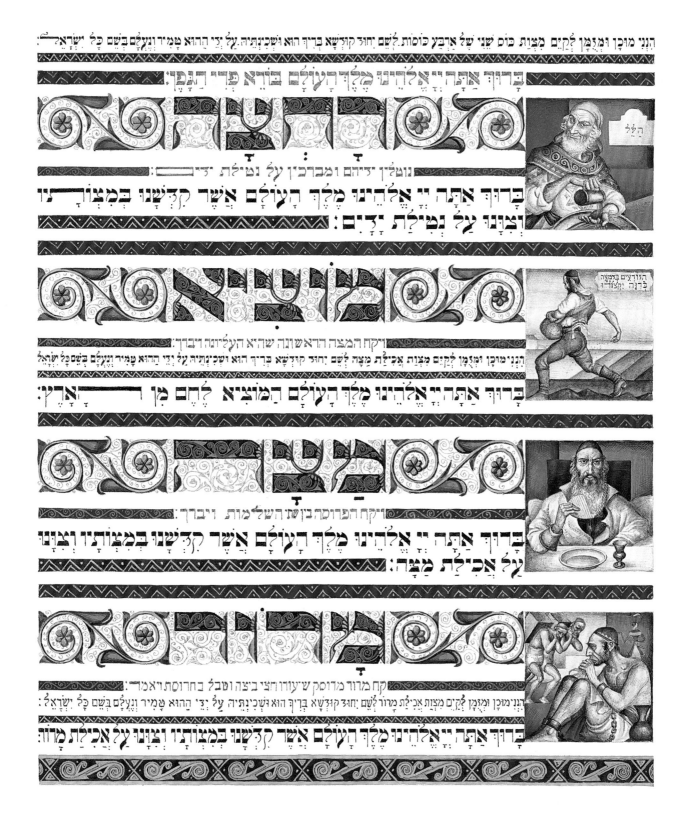

בָּרוּךְ אַתָּה יְיָ אֱלֹהֵינוּ מֶלֶךְ הָעוֹלָם בּוֹרֵא פְּרִי הַגָּפֶן.

נוֹטְלִין יְדֵיהֶם וּמְבָרְכִין עַל נְטִילַת יָדַיִם

בָּרוּךְ אַתָּה יְיָ אֱלֹהֵינוּ מֶלֶךְ הָעוֹלָם אֲשֶׁר קִדְּשָׁנוּ בְּמִצְוֹתָיו וְצִוָּנוּ עַל נְטִילַת יָדָיִם:

וַיִּקַּח הַמַּצָּה הָרִאשׁוֹנָה שֶׁהִיא הָעֶלְיוֹנָה וִיבָרֵךְ:

הִנְנִי מוּכָן וּמְזֻמָּן לְקַיֵּם מִצְוַת אֲכִילַת מַצָּה לְשֵׁם יִחוּד קוּדְשָׁא בְּרִיךְ הוּא וּשְׁכִינְתֵּיה עַל יְדֵי הַהוּא טָמִיר וְנֶעְלָם בְּשֵׁם כָּל יִשְׂרָאֵל

בָּרוּךְ אַתָּה אֱלֹהֵינוּ מֶלֶךְ הָעוֹלָם הַמּוֹצִיא לֶחֶם מִן הָאָרֶץ:

וַיִּקַּח הַפְּרוּסָה בֵּין שְׁתֵּי הַשְּׁלֵמוֹת וִיבָרֵךְ:

בָּרוּךְ אַתָּה יְיָ אֱלֹהֵינוּ מֶלֶךְ הָעוֹלָם אֲשֶׁר קִדְּשָׁנוּ בְּמִצְוֹתָיו וְצִוָּנוּ עַל אֲכִילַת מַצָּה:

קַח מָרוֹר מִדּוּסָק שֶׁיְּעוֹרֵר חֲצִי בֵּיצָה וְטֹבֵל בַּחֲרוֹסֶת וְיֹאמַר:

הִנְנִי מוּכָן וּמְזֻמָּן לְקַיֵּם מִצְוַת אֲכִילַת מָרוֹר לְשֵׁם יִחוּד קוּדְשָׁא בְּרִיךְ הוּא וּשְׁכִינְתֵּיה עַל יְדֵי הַהוּא טָמִיר וְנֶעְלָם בְּשֵׁם כָּל יִשְׂרָאֵל:

בָּרוּךְ אַתָּה יְיָ אֱלֹהֵינוּ מֶלֶךְ הָעוֹלָם אֲשֶׁר קִדְּשָׁנוּ בְּמִצְוֹתָיו וְצִוָּנוּ עַל אֲכִילַת מָרוֹר:

THE BLESSINGS BEFORE THE MEAL

The blessings before the meal begin with the blessing over the second of the four cups of wine of the Seder. We have not translated the kabbalistic meditations that Szyk added to this section; on these, see Commentary, pages 42, 44. In recent years, some people at this point in the Seder drink from the "Cup of Miriam" in commemoration of the role that Miriam and the Israelite women played in the redemption from Egypt; for more on this practice, see Commentary, pages 45–46.

Everyone then recites this blessing over the second cup of wine, while reclining to the left:

Blessed are you, Lord our God, Sovereign of the Universe, who creates the fruit of the vine. Barukh atah Adonai, Eloheinoo melekh ha-oh-lahm, boh-rei p'ree ha-gah-fen.

ROḤTZAH: *The Washing of the Hands*
In this sixth part of the Seder, all present wash their hands, and recite this blessing over the washing of hands:

Blessed are you, Lord our God, Sovereign of the Universe, who has sanctified us with his commandments, and has commanded us to perform the ritual of washing the hands.
Barukh atah Adonai, Eloheinoo melekh ha-oh-lahm, ah-sher kee-d'shah-noo b'meetz-voh-tav, v'tzee-vah-noo, al n'tee-laht yah-dy-yeem.

MOH-TZEE: *The Blessing Before the Meal*
In this seventh part of the Seder, someone takes the top matzah *and says the generic blessing over food:*

Blessed are you, Lord our God, Sovereign of the Universe, who brings forth bread from the earth. Barukh atah Adonai, Eloheinoo melekh ha-oh-lahm, ha-moh-tzee leḥem meen ha-ah-retz.

MATZAH
In this eighth part of the Seder, one takes portions from the remaining matzot *and says the following, after which one eats the* matzah:

Blessed are you, Lord our God, Sovereign of the Universe, who has sanctified us with his commandments, and has commanded us concerning the eating of *matzah.*
Barukh atah Adonai, Eloheinoo melekh ha-oh-lahm, ah-sher kee-d'shah-noo b'meetz-voh-tav, v'tzee-vah-noo, al ah-khee-laht matzah.

MAH-ROHR: *Bitter Herbs*
In this ninth part of the Seder, one takes some bitter herbs (about the size of a half of an egg), dips them in the ḥaroset, *and says:*

Blessed are you, Lord our God, Sovereign of the Universe, who has sanctified us with his commandments, and has commanded us concerning the eating of bitter herbs.
Barukh atah Adonai, Eloheinoo melekh ha-oh-lahm, ah-sher kee-d'shah-noo b'meetz-voh-tav, v'tzee-vah-noo, al ah-khee-laht mah-rohr.

It is Jewish practice to say grace after the meal, rather than before it. Nonetheless, before eating, certain blessings are recited over specific foods to be eaten. On Passover, such foods include matzah *and bitter herbs (see Exodus 12:8).*

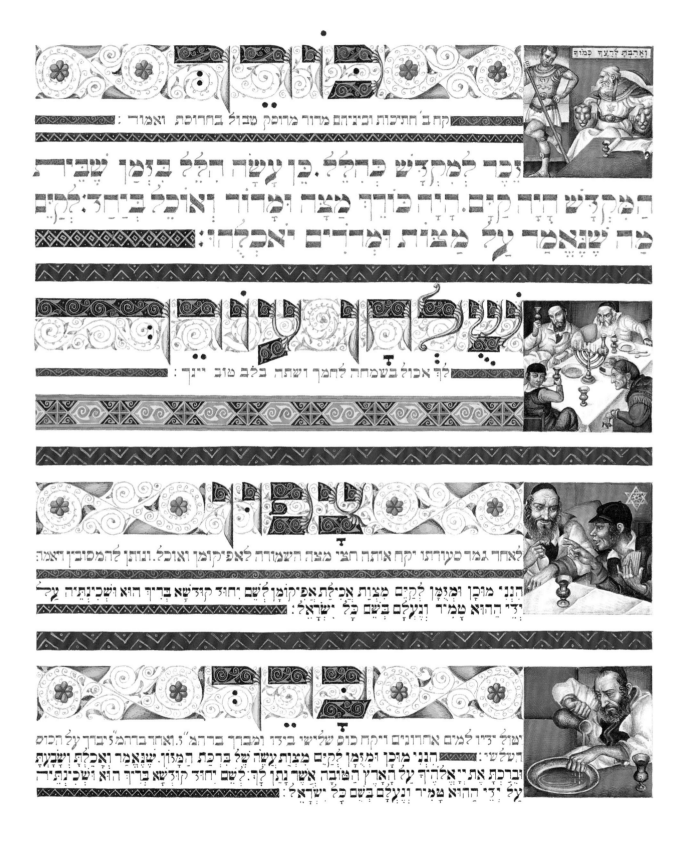

כֹּרֵךְ

קַח ב׳ חֲתִיכוֹת וּבֵינֵיהֶם מָרוֹר מְרֻסָּק טָבוּל בַּחֲרֹסֶת. וֶאֱמוֹר :

זֵכֶר לְמִקְדָּשׁ כְּהִלֵּל. כֵּן עָשָׂה הִלֵּל בִּזְמַן שֶׁבֵּית הַמִּקְדָּשׁ הָיָה קַיָּם. הָיָה כּוֹרֵךְ מַצָּה וּמָרוֹר וְאוֹכֵל בְּיַחַד. לְקַיֵּם מַה שֶּׁנֶּאֱמַר עַל מַצּוֹת וּמְרֹרִים יֹאכְלֻהוּ :

שֻׁלְחָן עוֹרֵךְ

לֶךְ אֱכֹל בְּשִׂמְחָה לַחְמֶךָ וּשְׁתֵה בְלֶב טוֹב יֵינֶךָ :

צָפוּן

לְאַחַר גְּמַר סְעוּדָתוֹ יִקַּח אוֹתָהּ חֲצִי מַצָּה הַשְּׁמוּרָה לָאֲפִיקוֹמָן וְאוֹכֵל. וְנוֹתֵן לְהַמְּסֻבִּין וְיֹאמַר :

הִנְנִי מוּכָן וּמְזֻמָּן לְקַיֵּם מִצְוַת אֲכִילַת אֲפִיקוֹמָן לְשֵׁם יִחוּד קוּדְשָׁא בְּרִיךְ הוּא וּשְׁכִינְתֵּיהּ עַל יְדֵי הַהוּא טָמִיר וְנֶעְלָם בְּשֵׁם כָּל יִשְׂרָאֵל :

בָּרֵךְ

יִטּוֹל יָדָיו לְמַיִם אַחֲרוֹנִים וְיִקַּח כּוֹס שְׁלִישִׁי בְּיָדוֹ וּמְבָרֵךְ בִּרְהַמָּ״ז. וְאֶחָד בְּרהמ״ז וְיִתְּבָרֵךְ עַל הַכּוֹס כָּל שֶׁהוּא : הִנְנִי מוּכָן וּמְזֻמָּן לְקַיֵּם מִצְוַת עֲשֵׂה שֶׁל בִּרְכַּת הַמָּזוֹן. שֶׁנֶּאֱמַר. וְאָכַלְתָּ וְשָׂבָעְתָּ וּבֵרַכְתָּ אֶת יְיָ אֱלֹהֶיךָ עַל הָאָרֶץ הַטּוֹבָה אֲשֶׁר נָתַן לָךְ. לְשֵׁם יִחוּד קוּדְשָׁא בְּרִיךְ הוּא וּשְׁכִינְתֵּיהּ עַל יְדֵי הַהוּא טָמִיר וְנֶעְלָם בְּשֵׁם כָּל יִשְׂרָאֵל :

KOREIKH: *The Combination*

The "Hillel sandwich" is first mentioned in early rabbinic literature (*Tosefta*, *Pesaḥim* 2:22). After it is eaten, the festive meal begins.

In this tenth part of the Seder, everyone takes two pieces of matzah, *places some bitter herbs (horseradish, lettuce, or both) that have already been dipped in* ḥaroset *between them, and recites the following before eating it. The blessings for* matzah *and bitter herbs already having been said, they need not be repeated. There is no particular blessing for the* ḥaroset.

[W]e do this] in commemoration of the Temple, and as a reminder of Hillel's practice. This is what Hillel would do when the Temple still stood. He would make a sandwich combining [the Paschal lamb,] *matzah*, and bitter herbs, and he would eat them together in fulfillment of the biblical verse, "with *matzot* and bitter herbs they shall eat it" ["it" here refers to the meat of the Passover sacrifice] (Exodus 12:8).

SHULḤAN OH-REIKH: *The "Set Table"*

This eleventh part of the Seder is everyone's favorite: the Passover feast. The menu for the Passover meal is largely determined by the place of familial origin. Jews of Polish, German, Yemenite, Persian, and other origins serve different kinds of foods for Passover, albeit within the guidelines of rabbinical law regarding what may be eaten during Passover. Among many Jews of eastern European heritage, it is customary to begin the meal with a cold "soup" of chopped eggs in saltwater, but in our cholesterol-conscious society, this custom is no longer widely observed.

TZAFOON: *The Hidden Matzah*

In this twelfth part of the Seder, which follows the festive meal, one takes the piece of matzah *earlier designated as the* Afikomen—dessert—and eats part of it. Then, one distributes a piece to each participant. Some delay eating the Afikomen *until the end of the Seder, after dessert has been served, since nothing is supposed to be eaten after eating the* Afikomen.

The *Afikomen* is hidden from the children, who must find it. Once it is found, the adults must "ransom" it from the children with the promise of a gift. This part of the Seder is called *Tzafoon*, or "hidden," because the *matzah* has been hidden. Eating the *Afikomen* is required by Talmudic law, and the Seder cannot conclude unless it has been eaten. On the meaning of "*Afikomen*," see Commentary, pages 32–33.

BAREIKH: *Grace After Meals*

Largely of ancient origin and mandated by Scripture (see Deuteronomy 8:10), the Grace After Meals is recited after every meal and is not unique to Passover. Grace After Meals constitutes the thirteenth part of the Seder. Szyk notes the kabbalistic custom of dipping one's fingers in water at the end of the meal. This custom is called the "latter waters." In what now follows, we have translated excerpts from the Grace After Meals. Grace begins with a call to prayer. Though not in *The Szyk Haggadah*, recitation of grace on festivals and the Sabbath is prefaced by singing or reciting Psalm 126, see Commentary, page 46; on "latter waters," see Commentary, page 44.

רַבּוֹתַי מִיר וֶוילֶן בֶּענְשֶׁן

יְהִי שֵׁם יְיָ מְבֹרָךְ מֵעַתָּה וְעַד עוֹלָם:
בִּרְשׁוּת מָרָנָן וְרַבּוֹתַי נְבָרֵךְ שֶׁאָכַלְנוּ מִשֶּׁלּוֹ:
בָּרוּךְ שֶׁאָכַלְנוּ מִשֶּׁלּוֹ וּבְטוּבוֹ חָיִינוּ:
בָּרוּךְ שֶׁאָכַלְנוּ מִשֶּׁלּוֹ וּבְטוּבוֹ חָיִינוּ:

בָּרוּךְ הוּא וּבָרוּךְ שְׁמוֹ:

בָּרוּךְ
אַתָּה יְיָ אֱלֹהֵינוּ מֶלֶךְ הָעוֹלָם הַזָּן אֶת הָעוֹלָם כֻּלּוֹ
בְּטוּבוֹ בְּחֵן בְּחֶסֶד וּבְרַחֲמִים הוּא נוֹתֵן לֶחֶם לְכָל
בָּשָׂר כִּי לְעוֹלָם חַסְדּוֹ. וּבְטוּבוֹ הַגָּדוֹל תָּמִיד לֹא
חָסַר לָנוּ וְאַל יֶחְסַר לָנוּ מָזוֹן לְעוֹלָם וָעֶד. בַּעֲבוּר
שְׁמוֹ הַגָּדוֹל. כִּי הוּא אֵל זָן וּמְפַרְנֵס לַכֹּל וּמֵטִיב
לַכֹּל וּמֵכִין מָזוֹן לְכָל בְּרִיּוֹתָיו אֲשֶׁר בָּרָא: בָּרוּךְ
אַתָּה יְיָ הַזָּן אֶת הַכֹּל:

נוֹדֶה לְּךָ יְיָ אֱלֹהֵינוּ עַל שֶׁהִנְחַלְתָּ לַאֲבוֹתֵינוּ אֶרֶץ חֶמְדָּה טוֹבָה
וּרְחָבָה וְעַל שֶׁהוֹצֵאתָנוּ יְיָ אֱלֹהֵינוּ מֵאֶרֶץ מִצְרַיִם וּפְדִיתָנוּ
מִבֵּית עֲבָדִים וְעַל בְּרִיתְךָ שֶׁחָתַמְתָּ בִּבְשָׂרֵנוּ וְעַל תּוֹרָתְךָ שֶׁלִּמַּדְתָּנוּ וְעַל חֻקֶּיךָ
שֶׁהוֹדַעְתָּנוּ וְעַל חַיִּים חֵן וָחֶסֶד שֶׁחוֹנַנְתָּנוּ וְעַל אֲכִילַת מָזוֹן שָׁאַתָּה
וּמְפַרְנֵס אוֹתָנוּ תָּמִיד בְּכָל יוֹם וּבְכָל עֵת וּבְכָל שָׁעָה:

וְעַל הַכֹּל יְיָ אֱלֹהֵינוּ אֲנַחְנוּ מוֹדִים לָךְ וּמְבָרְכִים אוֹתָךְ יִתְבָּרַךְ שִׁמְךָ
בְּפִי כָל חַי תָּמִיד לְעוֹלָם וָעֶד. כַּכָּתוּב וְאָכַלְתָּ וְשָׂבָעְתָּ וּבֵרַכְתָּ אֶת
יְיָ אֱלֹהֶיךָ עַל הָאָרֶץ הַטּוֹבָה אֲשֶׁר נָתַן לָךְ: בָּרוּךְ אַתָּה יְיָ עַל הָאָרֶץ וְעַל הַמָּזוֹן:

רַחֵם יְיָ אֱלֹהֵינוּ עַל יִשְׂרָאֵל עַמֶּךָ וְעַל יְרוּשָׁלַיִם עִירֶךָ
וְעַל צִיּוֹן מִשְׁכַּן כְּבוֹדֶךָ וְעַל מַלְכוּת בֵּית דָּוִד
מְשִׁיחֶךָ וְעַל הַבַּיִת הַגָּדוֹל וְהַקָּדוֹשׁ שֶׁנִּקְרָא שִׁמְךָ
עָלָיו. אֱלֹהֵינוּ אָבִינוּ רְעֵנוּ זוּנֵנוּ פַּרְנְסֵנוּ וְכַלְכְּלֵנוּ

Someone initiates the recitation of the Grace After Meals by asking:

Shall we say Grace?

Everyone responds:

May the Name of God be blessed now and for evermore.

The first person continues:

Then, with your permission, let us bless God of whose bounty we have eaten.

Everyone responds:

Blessed be God of whose bounty we have partaken, and through whose goodness our lives are sustained.

Everyone then says:

Blessed be God, and blessed be God's Name.

The Grace is now recited:

Blessed are you, Lord our God, who nourishes the entire world out of his goodness, with grace, love, and compassion. "Because God's steadfast love is eternal, he provides sustenance to all living things" (Psalms 136:25). Because of God's great goodness, we have never yet lacked for food. And, for the sake of God's great Name, may we never want for food in the future, for he is God who feeds and sustains all, who does good to all, and who provides nourishment to all his creatures, his creations. Blessed are you, God, who feeds all living creatures.

We thank you, Lord our God: for having granted our ancestors a lovely, good, and ample land [the Land of Israel]; for having brought us out of the land of Egypt; for having liberated us from bondage; for your covenant with us which is sealed upon our flesh [with circumcision]; for your Torah, in which you have instructed us; for your statutes that you have made known to us; for the gift of life, divine grace, and steadfast love that you have imparted unto us; and, for the nourishment by which you perpetually feed and sustain us—in every season, day, and hour.

For all this, Lord our God, we thank and bless you. May your Name be blessed by the mouths of all living things, perpetually and eternally, as it is written: "When you have eaten and are satisfied, you shall bless the Lord your God for the good land which he has given to you" (Deuteronomy 8:10). Blessed are you Lord for the land and for its sustenance.

NOTE: The text above and on the next page is an abridged translation of the Grace After Meals.

וְהַרְוִיחֵנוּ וְהַרְוַח לָנוּ יְיָ אֱלֹהֵינוּ מְהֵרָה מִכָּל צָרוֹתֵינוּ. וְנָא אַל תַּצְרִיכֵנוּ יְיָ
אֱלֹהֵינוּ לֹא לִידֵי מַתְּנַת בָּשָׂר וָדָם וְלֹא לִידֵי הַלְוָאָתָם כִּי אִם לְיָדְךָ
הַמְּלֵאָה הַפְּתוּחָה הַקְּדוֹשָׁה וְהָרְחָבָה שֶׁלֹּא נֵבוֹשׁ וְלֹא נִכָּלֵם לְעוֹלָם וָעֶד:

וְהַחֲלִיצֵנוּ יְיָ אֱלֹהֵינוּ בְּמִצְוֹתֶיךָ וּבְמִצְוַת יוֹם הַשְּׁבִיעִי הַשַּׁבָּת הַגָּדוֹל וְהַקָּדוֹשׁ הַזֶּה כִּי יוֹם זֶה גָּדוֹל
וְקָדוֹשׁ הוּא לְפָנֶיךָ לִשְׁבָּת בּוֹ וְלָנוּחַ בּוֹ בְּאַהֲבָה כְּמִצְוַת רְצוֹנֶךָ וּבִרְצוֹנְךָ הָנִיחַ לָנוּ יְיָ אֱלֹהֵינוּ שֶׁלֹּא
תְהֵא צָרָה וְיָגוֹן וַאֲנָחָה בְּיוֹם מְנוּחָתֵנוּ. וְהַרְאֵנוּ יְיָ אֱלֹהֵינוּ בְּנֶחָמַת צִיּוֹן עִירֶךָ וּבְבִנְיַן יְרוּשָׁלַיִם עִיר קָדְשֶׁךָ כִּי
אַתָּה הוּא בַּעַל הַיְשׁוּעוֹת וּבַעַל הַנֶּחָמוֹת:

וֵאלֹהֵי אֲבוֹתֵינוּ
יַעֲלֶה וְיָבֹא וְיַגִּיעַ
וְיֵרָאֶה וְיֵרָצֶה וְיִשָּׁמַע
וְיִפָּקֵד וְיִזָּכֵר זִכְרוֹנֵנוּ וּפִקְדוֹנֵנוּ וְזִכְרוֹן אֲבוֹתֵינוּ. וְזִכְרוֹן מָשִׁיחַ
בֶּן דָּוִד עַבְדֶּךָ. וְזִכְרוֹן יְרוּשָׁלַיִם עִיר קָדְשֶׁךָ. וְזִכְרוֹן כָּל עַמְּךָ
בֵּית יִשְׂרָאֵל לְפָנֶיךָ לִפְלֵיטָה לְטוֹבָה לְחֵן וּלְחֶסֶד וּלְרַחֲמִים
לְחַיִּים וּלְשָׁלוֹם בְּיוֹם חַג הַמַּצּוֹת הַזֶּה: זָכְרֵנוּ יְיָ אֱלֹהֵינוּ בּוֹ
לְטוֹבָה. וּפָקְדֵנוּ בוֹ לִבְרָכָה. וְהוֹשִׁיעֵנוּ בּוֹ לְחַיִּים. וּבִדְבַר
יְשׁוּעָה וְרַחֲמִים חוּס וְחָנֵּנוּ. וְרַחֵם עָלֵינוּ
וְהוֹשִׁיעֵנוּ. כִּי אֵלֶיךָ עֵינֵינוּ. כִּי
אֵל מֶלֶךְ חַנּוּן וְרַחוּם אָתָּה:

Our God and God of our ancestors: May there ascend, come, arrive, be seen, be desired, and be heard in your presence, the remembrance and recollection of us; and the remembrance of our forebears; the remembrance of your servant, the Messiah son of David; the remembrance of Jerusalem, your holy city; and the remembrance of all your people, the House of Israel. May all these be recalled for deliverance and for good, with grace and compassion, for life and for peace, on this day of the Festival of the *Matzot*. Remember us on this day, Lord, our God, for good. Designate this day for blessing, and save us on this day for life. With the promise of salvation and compassion, spare us; be gracious unto us; have mercy upon us, and save us. We look to you, since you are a gracious and merciful king.

עִיר הַקֹּדֶשׁ בִּמְהֵרָה בְיָמֵינוּ. בָּרוּךְ אַתָּה יְיָ בּוֹנֶה בְרַחֲמָיו יְרוּשָׁלָיִם. אָמֵן: בָּרוּךְ
אַתָּה יְיָ אֱלֹהֵינוּ מֶלֶךְ הָעוֹלָם הָאֵל אָבִינוּ מַלְכֵּנוּ אַדִּירֵנוּ בּוֹרְאֵנוּ גּוֹאֲלֵנוּ
יוֹצְרֵנוּ קְדוֹשֵׁנוּ קְדוֹשׁ יַעֲקֹב רוֹעֵנוּ רוֹעֵה יִשְׂרָאֵל הַמֶּלֶךְ הַטּוֹב וְהַמֵּטִיב לַכֹּל
שֶׁבְּכָל יוֹם וָיוֹם הוּא הֵטִיב. הוּא מֵטִיב. הוּא יֵיטִיב לָנוּ. הוּא גְמָלָנוּ הוּא
גוֹמְלֵנוּ הוּא יִגְמְלֵנוּ לָעַד לְחֵן וּלְחֶסֶד וּלְרַחֲמִים וּלְרֶוַח הַצָּלָה וְהַצְלָחָה
בְרָכָה וִישׁוּעָה נֶחָמָה פַּרְנָסָה וְכַלְכָּלָה וְרַחֲמִים וְחַיִּים וְשָׁלוֹם וְכָל טוֹב
וּמִכָּל טוּב לְעוֹלָם אַל יְחַסְּרֵנוּ: הָרַחֲמָן הוּא יִמְלוֹךְ עָלֵינוּ לְעוֹלָם וָעֶד:
הָרַחֲמָן הוּא יִתְבָּרַךְ בַּשָּׁמַיִם וּבָאָרֶץ: הָרַחֲמָן הוּא יִשְׁתַּבַּח לְדוֹר דּוֹרִים
וְיִתְפָּאַר בָּנוּ לָעַד וּלְנֵצַח נְצָחִים וְיִתְהַדַּר בָּנוּ לָעַד וּלְעוֹלְמֵי עוֹלָמִים:
הָרַחֲמָן הוּא יְפַרְנְסֵנוּ בְכָבוֹד: הָרַחֲמָן הוּא יִשְׁבּוֹר עֻלֵּנוּ מֵעַל צַוָּארֵנוּ
וְהוּא יוֹלִיכֵנוּ קוֹמְמִיּוּת לְאַרְצֵנוּ: הָרַחֲמָן הוּא יִשְׁלַח לָנוּ בְרָכָה מְרֻבָּה
בַּבַּיִת הַזֶּה וְעַל שֻׁלְחָן זֶה שֶׁאָכַלְנוּ עָלָיו: הָרַחֲמָן הוּא יִשְׁלַח לָנוּ אֶת
אֵלִיָּהוּ הַנָּבִיא זָכוּר לַטּוֹב וִיבַשֶּׂר לָנוּ בְשׂוֹרוֹת טוֹבוֹת יְשׁוּעוֹת וְנֶחָמוֹת:
הָרַחֲמָן הוּא יְבָרֵךְ אֶת אָבִי מוֹרִי בַּעַל הַבַּיִת הַזֶּה וְאֵת אִמִּי מוֹרָתִי
בַּעֲלַת הַבַּיִת הַזֶּה. אוֹתִי וְאֶת אִשְׁתִּי וְאֶת זַרְעִי וְאֶת כָּל אֲשֶׁר לִי. אוֹתָם
וְאֵת בֵּיתָם וְאֵת זַרְעָם וְאֵת כָּל אֲשֶׁר לָהֶם. אוֹתָנוּ וְאֵת כָּל אֲשֶׁר לָנוּ כְּמוֹ
שֶׁנִּתְבָּרְכוּ אֲבוֹתֵינוּ אַבְרָהָם יִצְחָק וְיַעֲקֹב בַּכֹּל מִכֹּל כֹּל כֵּן יְבָרֵךְ אוֹתָנוּ
כֻּלָּנוּ יַחַד בִּבְרָכָה שְׁלֵמָה וְנֹאמַר אָמֵן:

וְלָמְדוּ עָלָיו וְעָלֵינוּ זְכוּת שֶׁתְּהֵא לְמִשְׁמֶרֶת שָׁלוֹם וְנִשָּׂא בְרָכָה מֵאֵת יְיָ וּצְדָקָה
מֵאֱלֹהֵי יִשְׁעֵנוּ וְנִמְצָא חֵן וְשֵׂכֶל טוֹב בְּעֵינֵי אֱלֹהִים וְאָדָם:

לשבת

הָרַחֲמָן הוּא יַנְחִילֵנוּ לְיוֹם שֶׁכֻּלּוֹ עַצְבַת וּמְנוּחָה לְחַיֵּי הָעוֹלָמִים: הָרַחֲמָן הוּא יַנְחִילֵנוּ לְיוֹם שֶׁכֻּלּוֹ טוֹב:

הוּא יְזַכֵּנוּ לִימוֹת הַמָּשִׁיחַ וּלְחַיֵּי הָעוֹלָם הַבָּא: מִגְדּוֹל יְשׁוּעוֹת מַלְכּוֹ וְעֹשֶׂה חֶסֶד לִמְשִׁיחוֹ
לְדָוִד וּלְזַרְעוֹ עַד עוֹלָם: עֹשֶׂה שָׁלוֹם בִּמְרוֹמָיו הוּא יַעֲשֶׂה שָׁלוֹם עָלֵינוּ וְעַל כָּל יִשְׂרָאֵל
וְאִמְרוּ אָמֵן:

אֶת יְיָ קְדוֹשָׁיו כִּי אֵין מַחְסוֹר לִירֵאָיו: כְּפִירִים רָשׁוּ וְרָעֵבוּ וְדוֹרְשֵׁי יְיָ לֹא יַחְסְרוּ כָל טוֹב: הוֹדוּ לַיְיָ
כִּי טוֹב כִּי לְעוֹלָם חַסְדּוֹ: פּוֹתֵחַ אֶת יָדֶךָ וּמַשְׂבִּיעַ לְכָל חַי רָצוֹן: בָּרוּךְ הַגֶּבֶר אֲשֶׁר יִבְטַח בַּיְיָ וְהָיָה יְיָ
מִבְטַחוֹ: נַעַר הָיִיתִי גַּם זָקַנְתִּי וְלֹא רָאִיתִי צַדִּיק נֶעֱזָב וְזַרְעוֹ מְבַקֶּשׁ לָחֶם: יְיָ עֹז לְעַמּוֹ יִתֵּן יְיָ יְבָרֵךְ אֶת עַמּוֹ בַשָּׁלוֹם:

הִנְנִי מוּכָן וּמְזֻמָּן לְקַיֵּם מִצְוַת כּוֹס שְׁלִישִׁי מֵאַרְבַּע כּוֹסוֹת לְשֵׁם יִחוּד קוּדְשָׁא בְּרִיךְ הוּא וּשְׁכִינְתֵּיהּ עַל יְדֵי הַהוּא טָמִיר וְנֶעְלָם בְּשֵׁם כָּל יִשְׂרָאֵל:

בָּרוּךְ אַתָּה יְיָ אֱלֹהֵינוּ מֶלֶךְ הָעוֹלָם בּוֹרֵא פְּרִי הַגָּפֶן:

Rebuild Jerusalem—the sacred city, speedily, and in our days. Blessed are you God, who in his mercy, rebuilds Jerusalem.

All respond: **Amen.**

May the Merciful One rule over us forever and ever!

All respond: **Amen.**

May the Merciful One be blessed in heaven and on the earth!

All respond: **Amen.**

May the Merciful One be praised from generation to generation, glorified by us throughout all eternity and honored by us for all time!

All respond: **Amen.**

May the Merciful One sustain us for all time!

All respond: **Amen.**

May the Merciful One sustain us with an honorable livelihood!

All respond: **Amen.**

May the Merciful One shatter the yoke of oppression from around our necks, and lead us in upright dignity to our land!

All respond: **Amen.**

May the Merciful One bestow manifold blessings upon this home, and upon all those who have eaten at this table!

All respond: **Amen.**

May the merit of our ancestors in heaven engender enduring peace.

All respond: **Amen.**

May we receive God's blessing and righteousness from the Lord who brings us deliverance. And, may we find favor and understanding in the eyes of God and our fellow human beings.

All respond: **Amen.**

(On the Sabbath, add:) **May the Merciful One grant us a day that will be a total Sabbath, [that is, the World to Come,] with eternal repose!**

All respond: **Amen.**

(Otherwise continue:) **May the Merciful One bestow upon us a day that is replete with goodness!**

All respond: **Amen.**

May the Merciful One grant us the privilege to witness messianic redemption and eternal life in the World-to-Come!

All respond: **Amen.**

"God is a tower of salvation to his kingship. He deals graciously with his anointed—with David and his offspring, forevermore" (2 Samuel 22:51).

May the maker of peace in the heavens also make peace upon us, all the people of Israel, to which we say: Amen.

Grace After Meals ends with the blessing over the third of the four cups of wine,
which all drink after reciting the following blessing while reclining to the left:

Blessed are you, Lord our God, Sovereign of the Universe, who creates the fruit of the vine.

Barukh atah Adonai, Eloheinoo melekh ha-oh-lahm, boh-rei p'ree ha-gah-fen.

שְׁפֹךְ חֲמָתְךָ אֶל הַגּוֹיִם אֲשֶׁר לֹא
יְדָעוּךָ וְעַל מַמְלָכוֹת אֲשֶׁר

בְּשִׁמְךָ לֹא קָרָאוּ: כִּי אָכַל אֶת
יַעֲקֹב וְאֶת נָוֵהוּ הֵשַׁמּוּ: שְׁפָךְ
עֲלֵיהֶם זַעְמֶךָ וַחֲרוֹן אַפְּךָ יַשִּׂיגֵם:
תִּרְדֹּף בְּאַף וְתַשְׁמִידֵם מִתַּחַת שְׁמֵי יְיָ:

JUST RETRIBUTION

The Elijah Cup is filled. It is customary to open the front door. A song welcoming Elijah is customarily sung as all watch for Elijah to enter and to drink from his cup. On the Elijah Cup, see Commentary, page 18.

Ei-lee-yahoo ha-nah-vee, Ei-lee-yahoo ha-teesh-bee, Ei-lee-yahoo, Ei-lee-yahoo, Ei-lee-yahoo ha-gee-lah-dee. Beem-hei-rah b'yah-mei-noo yah-voh ei-lei-noo, eem mah-shee-aḥ ben daveed, eem mah-shee-aḥ ben daveed. Ei-lee-yahoo ha-nah-vee, Ei-lee-yahoo ha-teesh-bee.

[Elijah the prophet—Elijah the Tishbite—may he soon come to us with the Messiah son of David; Elijah the prophet, Elijah the Tishbite.]

Elijah, the biblical prophet, is considered a harbinger of messianic redemption, which completes the redemptive process initiated with the Exodus from Egypt. As Elijah is welcomed into our homes and to our Seder, the following biblical verses are recited calling upon God to visit just vengeance upon the enemies of Israel as part of the process of bringing redemption, just as God did at the redemption from Egypt. The custom of reciting these verses was introduced during the Middle Ages by German Jews who were suffering severe persecution during the Crusades. On redemption and retribution, see Commentary, pages 33–36, 40, 42.

Pour out your wrath upon the nations that do not know you, and upon the kingdoms that do not invoke your Name, for they have devoured Jacob and have laid waste his home. Pour out your fury against them. May your blazing anger overtake them. Pursue them in anger and destroy them from under the heavens of the Lord! (Psalms 79:6–7; Psalms 69:25; Lamentations 3:66).

לָנוּ יְיָ לֹא לָנוּ כִּי לְשִׁמְךָ תֵּן כָּבוֹד עַל חַסְדְּךָ עַל אֲמִתֶּךָ: לָמָּה יֹאמְרוּ הַגּוֹיִם אַיֵּה נָא
אֱלֹהֵיהֶם: וֵאלֹהֵינוּ בַשָּׁמָיִם כֹּל אֲשֶׁר חָפֵץ עָשָׂה: עֲצַבֵּיהֶם כֶּסֶף וְזָהָב מַעֲשֵׂה יְדֵי אָדָם:
פֶּה לָהֶם וְלֹא יְדַבֵּרוּ עֵינַיִם לָהֶם וְלֹא יִרְאוּ: אָזְנַיִם לָהֶם וְלֹא יִשְׁמָעוּ אַף לָהֶם וְלֹא
יְרִיחוּן: יְדֵיהֶם וְלֹא יְמִישׁוּן רַגְלֵיהֶם וְלֹא יְהַלֵּכוּ לֹא יֶהְגּוּ בִּגְרוֹנָם: כְּמוֹהֶם יִהְיוּ
עֹשֵׂיהֶם כֹּל אֲשֶׁר בֹּטֵחַ בָּהֶם: יִשְׂרָאֵל בְּטַח בַּיְיָ עֶזְרָם וּמָגִנָּם הוּא: בֵּית אַהֲרֹן בִּטְחוּ
בַיְיָ עֶזְרָם וּמָגִנָּם הוּא: יִרְאֵי יְיָ בִּטְחוּ בַיְיָ עֶזְרָם וּמָגִנָּם הוּא:

יְיָ זְכָרָנוּ יְבָרֵךְ יְבָרֵךְ אֶת בֵּית יִשְׂרָאֵל
יְבָרֵךְ אֶת בֵּית אַהֲרֹן: יְבָרֵךְ יִרְאֵי יְיָ הַקְּטַנִּים עִם הַגְּדֹלִים:
יֹסֵף יְיָ עֲלֵיכֶם וְעַל בְּנֵיכֶם: בְּרוּכִים אַתֶּם לַיְיָ עֹשֵׂה
שָׁמַיִם וָאָרֶץ: הַשָּׁמַיִם שָׁמַיִם לַיְיָ וְהָאָרֶץ נָתַן לִבְנֵי אָדָם: לֹא
הַמֵּתִים יְהַלְלוּ יָהּ וְלֹא כָּל יֹרְדֵי דוּמָה: וַאֲנַחְנוּ נְבָרֵךְ יָהּ מֵעַתָּה וְעַד עוֹלָם הַלְלוּיָהּ:

אָהַבְתִּי כִּי יִשְׁמַע יְיָ אֶת קוֹלִי תַּחֲנוּנָי: כִּי הִטָּה אָזְנוֹ לִי וּבְיָמַי אֶקְרָא: אֲפָפוּנִי חֶבְלֵי מָוֶת וּמְצָרֵי
שְׁאוֹל מְצָאוּנִי צָרָה וְיָגוֹן אֶמְצָא: וּבְשֵׁם יְיָ אֶקְרָא אָנָּה יְיָ מַלְּטָה נַפְשִׁי: חַנּוּן יְיָ וְצַדִּיק
וֵאלֹהֵינוּ מְרַחֵם: שֹׁמֵר פְּתָאיִם יְיָ דַּלֹּתִי וְלִי יְהוֹשִׁיעַ: שׁוּבִי נַפְשִׁי לִמְנוּחָיְכִי כִּי יְיָ גָּמַל עָלָיְכִי: כִּי חִלַּצְתָּ נַפְשִׁי
מִמָּוֶת אֶת עֵינִי מִן דִּמְעָה אֶת רַגְלִי מִדֶּחִי: אֶתְהַלֵּךְ לִפְנֵי יְיָ בְּאַרְצוֹת הַחַיִּים: הֶאֱמַנְתִּי כִּי אֲדַבֵּר אֲנִי עָנִיתִי מְאֹד: אֲנִי אָמַרְתִּי
בְחָפְזִי כָּל הָאָדָם כֹּזֵב:

מָה אָשִׁיב לַיְיָ כָּל תַּגְמוּלוֹהִי עָלָי: כּוֹס יְשׁוּעוֹת אֶשָּׂא
וּבְשֵׁם יְיָ אֶקְרָא: נְדָרַי לַיְיָ אֲשַׁלֵּם נֶגְדָה נָּא לְכָל עַמּוֹ:
יָקָר בְּעֵינֵי יְיָ הַמָּוְתָה לַחֲסִידָיו: אָנָּה יְיָ כִּי אֲנִי
עַבְדֶּךָ אֲנִי עַבְדְּךָ בֶּן אֲמָתֶךָ פִּתַּחְתָּ לְמוֹסֵרָי:
לְךָ אֶזְבַּח זֶבַח תּוֹדָה וּבְשֵׁם יְיָ אֶקְרָא: נְדָרַי לַיְיָ
אֲשַׁלֵּם נֶגְדָה נָּא לְכָל עַמּוֹ: בְּחַצְרוֹת בֵּית יְיָ בְּתוֹכֵכִי יְרוּשָׁלָיִם הַלְלוּיָהּ:

הַלְלוּ אֶת יְיָ כָּל גּוֹיִם שַׁבְּחוּהוּ כָּל הָאֻמִּים: כִּי גָבַר עָלֵינוּ חַסְדּוֹ וֶאֱמֶת יְיָ לְעוֹלָם הַלְלוּיָהּ:

הוֹדוּ לַיְיָ כִּי טוֹב כִּי לְעוֹלָם חַסְדּוֹ:
יֹאמַר נָא יִשְׂרָאֵל כִּי לְעוֹלָם חַסְדּוֹ:
יֹאמְרוּ נָא בֵּית אַהֲרֹן כִּי לְעוֹלָם חַסְדּוֹ:
יֹאמְרוּ נָא יִרְאֵי יְיָ כִּי לְעוֹלָם חַסְדּוֹ:

HALLEIL: Psalms of Praise

Reciting psalms has been a feature of observance of the night of Passover since ancient times. Psalms were said in the Temple when pilgrims came there for Passover. Already by the first century, we know that people who could not make the pilgrimage to the Temple went to the synagogue the night of the Seder to recite them. Eventually, the custom of saying those psalms that together constitute the *Halleil*, recited as part of the liturgy on other holidays as well, was recited at the Seder—some psalms before the meal and others after the meal. The following psalms of *Halleil* represent the fourteenth part of the Seder. Note, however, that unlike usual recitations of the *Halleil* where a blessing is recited, no blessing before reciting the *Halleil* is recited at the Seder. In the Hebrew text, you will find Psalms 115–18 and Psalm 136 (called "The Great *Halleil*," although it is not part of the *Halleil*). In English translation are excerpts from these psalms, beginning with Psalms 117 and 118 (bottom right):

PSALM 117

Praise the Lord, all you nations.
Extol him, all you peoples.
For great is his love for us; God's truth is eternal. *Halleluyah*—**Praise God!**

Psalm 118: 1–4 may be read responsively in English:

PSALM 118: 1–4

Thank God for he is good:
His love is eternal.
Let Israel declare:
"His love is eternal."
Let the House of Aaron declare:
"His love is eternal."
Let those in awe of God declare:
"His love is eternal."

הַמֵּצַר קָרָאתִי יָהּ עָנָנִי בַמֶּרְחָב יָהּ: יְיָ לִי לֹא אִירָא מַה יַעֲשֶׂה לִי אָדָם: יְיָ לִי בְּעֹזְרָי
וַאֲנִי אֶרְאֶה בְּשֹׂנְאָי: טוֹב לַחֲסוֹת בַּיְיָ מִבְּטֹחַ בָּאָדָם: טוֹב לַחֲסוֹת בַּיְיָ מִבְּטֹחַ
בִּנְדִיבִים: כָּל גּוֹיִם סְבָבוּנִי בְּשֵׁם יְיָ כִּי אֲמִילַם: סַבּוּנִי גַם סְבָבוּנִי בְּשֵׁם יְיָ כִּי אֲמִילַם:
סַבּוּנִי כִדְבֹרִים דֹּעֲכוּ כְּאֵשׁ קוֹצִים בְּשֵׁם יְיָ כִּי אֲמִילַם: דָּחֹה דְחִיתַנִי לִנְפֹּל וַיְיָ עֲזָרָנִי: עָזִּי
וְזִמְרָת יָהּ וַיְהִי לִי לִישׁוּעָה: קוֹל רִנָּה וִישׁוּעָה בְּאָהֳלֵי צַדִּיקִים יְמִין יְיָ עֹשָׂה חָיִל:
יְמִין יְיָ רוֹמֵמָה יְמִין יְיָ עֹשָׂה חָיִל: לֹא אָמוּת כִּי אֶחְיֶה וַאֲסַפֵּר מַעֲשֵׂי יָהּ: יַסֹּר יִסְּרַנִּי יָּהּ
וְלַמָּוֶת לֹא נְתָנָנִי: פִּתְחוּ לִי שַׁעֲרֵי צֶדֶק אָבֹא בָם אוֹדֶה יָהּ: זֶה הַשַּׁעַר לַיְיָ צַדִּיקִים יָבֹאוּ
בוֹ: אוֹדְךָ כִּי עֲנִיתָנִי וַתְּהִי לִי לִישׁוּעָה: אֶבֶן מָאֲסוּ הַבּוֹנִים הָיְתָה לְרֹאשׁ פִּנָּה: מֵאֵת יְיָ הָיְתָה זֹּאת הִיא
נִפְלָאת בְּעֵינֵינוּ: זֶה הַיּוֹם עָשָׂה יְיָ נָגִילָה וְנִשְׂמְחָה בוֹ: זֶה

אָנָּא יְיָ   הוֹשִׁיעָה נָּא:
אָנָּא יְיָ   הוֹשִׁיעָה נָּא:
אָנָּא יְיָ   הַצְלִיחָה נָא:
אָנָּא יְיָ   הַצְלִיחָה נָא:

וַיֹּאמֶר יְיָ אֶל בָּב
נָה אֲדָמָה לַיְיָ
בְּעֵמֶק מָד דַּ

בָּרוּךְ הַבָּא בְּשֵׁם יְיָ בֵּרַכְנוּכֶם מִבֵּית יְיָ: אֵל יְיָ וַיָּאֶר לָנוּ אִסְרוּ חַג בַּעֲבֹתִים עַד קַרְנוֹת הַמִּזְבֵּחַ: אֵל
אֵלִי אַתָּה וְאוֹדֶךָּ אֱלֹהַי אֲרוֹמְמֶךָּ: הוֹדוּ לַיְיָ כִּי טוֹב כִּי לְעוֹלָם חַסְדּוֹ: הוֹדוּ

PSALM 118: 25

O Lord, we implore you, save us!

O Lord, we implore you, save us!

O Lord, we implore you, let us prosper!

O Lord, we implore you, let us prosper!

רֵאשִׁית גּוֹיִם עֲמָלֵק וְאַחֲרִיתוֹ עֲדֵי אֹבֵד

הוֹדוּ לַיְיָ כִּי טוֹב
הוֹדוּ לֵאלֹהֵי הָאֱלֹהִים
הוֹדוּ לַאֲדֹנֵי הָאֲדֹנִים
לְעֹשֵׂה נִפְלָאוֹת גְּדֹלוֹת לְבַדּוֹ
לְעֹשֵׂה הַשָּׁמַיִם בִּתְבוּנָה
לְרֹקַע הָאָרֶץ עַל הַמָּיִם
לְעֹשֵׂה אוֹרִים גְּדֹלִים
אֶת הַשֶּׁמֶשׁ לְמֶמְשֶׁלֶת בַּיּוֹם
אֶת הַיָּרֵחַ וְכוֹכָבִים לְמֶמְשְׁלוֹת בַּלָּיְלָה
לְמַכֵּה מִצְרַיִם בִּבְכוֹרֵיהֶם
וַיּוֹצֵא יִשְׂרָאֵל מִתּוֹכָם
בְּיָד חֲזָקָה וּבִזְרוֹעַ נְטוּיָה
לְגֹזֵר יַם סוּף לִגְזָרִים
וְהֶעֱבִיר יִשְׂרָאֵל בְּתוֹכוֹ
וְנִעֵר פַּרְעֹה וְחֵילוֹ בְיַם סוּף
לְמוֹלִיךְ עַמּוֹ בַּמִּדְבָּר
לְמַכֵּה מְלָכִים גְּדֹלִים
וַיַּהֲרֹג מְלָכִים אַדִּירִים
לְסִיחוֹן מֶלֶךְ הָאֱמֹרִי
וּלְעוֹג מֶלֶךְ הַבָּשָׁן
וְנָתַן אַרְצָם לְנַחֲלָה
נַחֲלָה לְיִשְׂרָאֵל עַבְדּוֹ
שֶׁבְּשִׁפְלֵנוּ זָכַר לָנוּ
וַיִּפְרְקֵנוּ מִצָּרֵינוּ
נֹתֵן לֶחֶם לְכָל בָּשָׂר
הוֹדוּ לְאֵל הַשָּׁמָיִם

לְעוֹלָם חַסְדּוֹ
לְעוֹלָם חַסְדּוֹ
לְעוֹלָם חַסְדּוֹ
לְעוֹלָם חַסְדּוֹ
לְעוֹלָם חַסְדּוֹ
לְעוֹלָם חַסְדּוֹ
לְעוֹלָם חַסְדּוֹ
לְעוֹלָם חַסְדּוֹ
לְעוֹלָם חַסְדּוֹ
לְעוֹלָם חַסְדּוֹ
לְעוֹלָם חַסְדּוֹ
לְעוֹלָם חַסְדּוֹ
לְעוֹלָם חַסְדּוֹ
לְעוֹלָם חַסְדּוֹ
לְעוֹלָם חַסְדּוֹ
לְעוֹלָם חַסְדּוֹ
לְעוֹלָם חַסְדּוֹ
לְעוֹלָם חַסְדּוֹ
לְעוֹלָם חַסְדּוֹ
לְעוֹלָם חַסְדּוֹ
לְעוֹלָם חַסְדּוֹ
לְעוֹלָם חַסְדּוֹ
לְעוֹלָם חַסְדּוֹ
לְעוֹלָם חַסְדּוֹ
לְעוֹלָם חַסְדּוֹ
לְעוֹלָם חַסְדּוֹ

Excerpts from Psalm 136 may be read responsively with the Hebrew and/or English refrains:

Kee l'oh-lahm ḥas-doh.
For his love is eternal.

PSALM 136

Thank God, for he is good:	*For his love is eternal.*
Praise God, supremely divine:	*Kee l'oh-lahm ḥas-doh.*
Praise God, the supreme Lord:	*For his love is eternal.*
Who alone works great wonders:	*Kee l'oh-lahm ḥas-doh.*
Who made the heavens with wisdom:	*For his love is eternal. . . .*
Who smote the firstborn of Egypt:	*Kee l'oh-lahm ḥas-doh.*
And, who brought Israel out of their midst:	*For his love is eternal.*
With a strong hand and an outstretched arm:	*Kee l'oh-lahm ḥas-doh.*
Who parted the Sea of Reeds:	*For his love is eternal.*
And, who allowed Israel to pass through it:	*Kee l'oh-lahm-ḥas-doh.*
But who cast Pharaoh and his army into the Sea of Reeds:	*For his love is eternal.*
Who led his people Israel through the wilderness:	*Kee l'oh-lahm ḥas-doh.*
Who struck down mighty kings:	*For his love is eternal. . . .*
Who remembered us in our afflictions:	*Kee l'oh-lahm ḥas-doh.*
And, who rescued us from our enemies:	*For his love is eternal.*
Who provides food for all creatures:	*Kee l'oh-lahm ḥas-doh.*
Thank the God of heaven:	*For his love is eternal!*

תְּבָרֵךְ אֶת שִׁמְךָ יְיָ אֱלֹהֵינוּ וְרוּחַ כָּל בָּשָׂר תְּפָאֵר וּתְרוֹמֵם זִכְרְךָ מַלְכֵּנוּ תָּמִיד. מִן
הָעוֹלָם וְעַד הָעוֹלָם אַתָּה אֵל וּמִבַּלְעָדֶיךָ אֵין לָנוּ מֶלֶךְ גּוֹאֵל וּמוֹשִׁיעַ. פּוֹדֶה וּמַצִּיל וּמְפַרְנֵס
וּמְרַחֵם בְּכָל עֵת צָרָה וְצוּקָה. אֵין לָנוּ מֶלֶךְ אֶלָּא אָתָּה. אֱלֹהֵי הָרִאשׁוֹנִים וְהָאַחֲרוֹנִים
אֱלוֹהַּ כָּל בְּרִיּוֹת. אֲדוֹן כָּל תּוֹלָדוֹת. הַמְהֻלָּל בְּרֹב הַתִּשְׁבָּחוֹת. הַמְנַהֵג עוֹלָמוֹ בְּחֶסֶד
וּבְרִיּוֹתָיו בְּרַחֲמִים. וַיְיָ לֹא יָנוּם וְלֹא יִישָׁן. הַמְעוֹרֵר יְשֵׁנִים וְהַמֵּקִיץ נִרְדָּמִים וְהַמֵּשִׂיחַ
אִלְּמִים וְהַמַּתִּיר אֲסוּרִים וְהַסּוֹמֵךְ נוֹפְלִים וְהַזּוֹקֵף כְּפוּפִים. לְךָ לְבַדְּךָ אֲנַחְנוּ מוֹדִים
אִלּוּ פִינוּ מָלֵא שִׁירָה כַּיָּם וּלְשׁוֹנֵנוּ רִנָּה כַּהֲמוֹן גַּלָּיו וְשִׂפְתוֹתֵינוּ שֶׁבַח כְּמֶרְחֲבֵי רָקִיעַ
וְעֵינֵינוּ מְאִירוֹת כַּשֶּׁמֶשׁ וְכַיָּרֵחַ וְיָדֵינוּ פְרוּשׂוֹת כְּנִשְׁרֵי שָׁמַיִם וְרַגְלֵינוּ קַלּוֹת כָּאַיָּלוֹת
אֵין אֲנַחְנוּ מַסְפִּיקִים לְהוֹדוֹת לְךָ יְיָ אֱלֹהֵינוּ וֵאלֹהֵי אֲבוֹתֵינוּ וּלְבָרֵךְ אֶת שְׁמֶךָ עַל אַחַת
מֵאָלֶף אֶלֶף אַלְפֵי אֲלָפִים וְרִבֵּי רְבָבוֹת פְּעָמִים הַטּוֹבוֹת שֶׁעָשִׂיתָ עִם אֲבוֹתֵינוּ וְעִמָּנוּ
מִמִּצְרַיִם גְּאַלְתָּנוּ יְיָ אֱלֹהֵינוּ וּמִבֵּית עֲבָדִים פְּדִיתָנוּ. בְּרָעָב זַנְתָּנוּ וּבְשָׂבָע כִּלְכַּלְתָּנוּ
מֵחֶרֶב הִצַּלְתָּנוּ וּמִדֶּבֶר מִלַּטְתָּנוּ וּמֵחֳלָיִם רָעִים וְנֶאֱמָנִים דִּלִּיתָנוּ. עַד הֵנָּה עֲזָרוּנוּ
רַחֲמֶיךָ וְלֹא עֲזָבוּנוּ חֲסָדֶיךָ. וְאַל תִּטְּשֵׁנוּ יְיָ אֱלֹהֵינוּ לָנֶצַח. עַל כֵּן אֵבָרִים שֶׁפִּלַּגְתָּ בָּנוּ
וְרוּחַ וּנְשָׁמָה שֶׁנָּפַחְתָּ בְּאַפֵּינוּ וְלָשׁוֹן אֲשֶׁר שַׂמְתָּ בְּפִינוּ. הֵן הֵם יוֹדוּ וִיבָרְכוּ וִישַׁבְּחוּ
וִיפָאֲרוּ וִירוֹמְמוּ וְיַעֲרִיצוּ וְיַקְדִּישׁוּ וְיַמְלִיכוּ אֶת שִׁמְךָ מַלְכֵּנוּ. כִּי כָל פֶּה לְךָ יוֹדֶה.
וְכָל לָשׁוֹן לְךָ תִשָּׁבַע. וְכָל בֶּרֶךְ לְךָ תִכְרַע. וְכָל קוֹמָה לְפָנֶיךָ תִשְׁתַּחֲוֶה. וְכָל לְבָבוֹת
יִירָאוּךָ וְכָל קֶרֶב וּכְלָיוֹת יְזַמְּרוּ לִשְׁמֶךָ. כַּדָּבָר שֶׁכָּתוּב כָּל עַצְמוֹתַי תֹּאמַרְנָה יְיָ
מִי כָמוֹךָ. מַצִּיל עָנִי מֵחָזָק מִמֶּנּוּ וְעָנִי וְאֶבְיוֹן מִגֹּזְלוֹ. מִי יִדְמֶה לָּךְ וּמִי יִשְׁוֶה לָּךְ
וּמִי יַעֲרָךְ לָךְ. הָאֵל הַגָּדוֹל הַגִּבּוֹר וְהַנּוֹרָא אֵל עֶלְיוֹן קוֹנֵה שָׁמַיִם וָאָרֶץ. נְהַלֶּלְךָ
וּנְשַׁבֵּחֲךָ וּנְפָאֶרְךָ וּנְבָרֵךְ אֶת שֵׁם קָדְשֶׁךָ כָּאָמוּר. לְדָוִד בָּרְכִי נַפְשִׁי אֶת יְיָ וְכָל קְרָבַי
אֶת שֵׁם קָדְשׁוֹ: הָאֵל בְּתַעֲצֻמוֹת עֻזֶּךָ. הַגָּדוֹל בִּכְבוֹד שְׁמֶךָ. הַגִּבּוֹר לָנֶצַח וְהַנּוֹרָא בְּנוֹרְאוֹתֶיךָ.
הַמֶּלֶךְ הַיּוֹשֵׁב עַל כִּסֵּא רָם וְנִשָּׂא

NISHMAT

An ancient prayer of unknown authorship, *Nishmat* and the prayers that serve as an addendum to it are written in a beautiful Hebrew poetic prose. Also part of the liturgy for Sabbath and festival mornings, these prayers continue the themes of the psalms that precede them, offering effusive praise of God, and beseeching his help in contending with the trials and tribulations of life. Excerpts from these prayers are translated below.

Even were our mouths full of song like the [sound of the] sea, our tongues as full of rejoicing as the multitudes of its waves, our lips as full of praise as the expanse of the horizon; though our eyes radiated light like the sun and the moon, and even if our hands could reach upward to heaven like the wings of eagles, and our feet were as swift as gazelles, our ability to praise you would still be inadequate—Lord, our God, and God of our ancestors—for the purpose of blessing your Name for even a single one of the countless plentitudes of the bounties that you have bestowed upon our forebears and upon us!

Lord our God, you have redeemed us from Egypt, and have delivered us from the house of bondage. In times of famine, you fed us; in times of plenty, you maintained us. From the sword, you rescued us, and from the plague you saved us. From life-threatening and from chronic diseases, you have relieved us. Up to this very moment, your compassion has helped us, and your love has never abandoned us. Lord, our God, may you never forsake us! Therefore, may the limbs that you have placed in our bodies, along with the spirit and the soul that you have infused within us, and the tongue that you set in our mouths; all thank, bless, praise, glorify, and sanctify you while proclaiming your sovereign title, O our king!

עַד מָרוֹם וְקָדוֹשׁ שְׁמוֹ. וְכַתוּב רַנְּנוּ צַדִּיקִים בַּיָי לַיְשָׁרִים נָאוָה תְהִלָּה: בְּפִי
יְשָׁרִים תִּתְהַלָּל. וּבְדִבְרֵי צַדִּיקִים תִּתְבָּרַךְ. וּבִלְשׁוֹן חֲסִידִים תִּתְרוֹמָם. וּבְקֶרֶב
קְדוֹשִׁים תִּתְקַדָּשׁ:

וּבְמַקְהֲלוֹת רִבְבוֹת עַמְּךָ בֵּית יִשְׂרָאֵל בְּרִנָּה יִתְפָּאַר שִׁמְךָ
מַלְכֵּנוּ בְּכָל דּוֹר וָדוֹר שֶׁכֵּן חוֹבַת כָּל הַיְצוּרִים
לְפָנֶיךָ יְיָ אֱלֹהֵינוּ וֵאלֹהֵי אֲבוֹתֵינוּ לְהוֹדוֹת לְהַלֵּל לְשַׁבֵּחַ לְפָאֵר לְרוֹמֵם לְהַדֵּר לְבָרֵךְ
לְעַלֵּה וּלְקַלֵּס עַל כָּל דִּבְרֵי שִׁירוֹת וְתִשְׁבָּחוֹת דָּוִד בֶּן יִשַׁי עַבְדְּךָ מְשִׁיחֶךָ:

יִשְׁתַּבַּח שִׁמְךָ לָעַד מַלְכֵּנוּ הָאֵל הַמֶּלֶךְ הַגָּדוֹל וְהַקָּדוֹשׁ בַּשָּׁמַיִם
וּבָאָרֶץ. כִּי לְךָ נָאֶה יְיָ אֱלֹהֵינוּ וֵאלֹהֵי אֲבוֹתֵינוּ שִׁיר וּשְׁבָחָה הַלֵּל וְזִמְרָה עֹז
וּמֶמְשָׁלָה נֶצַח גְּדֻלָּה וּגְבוּרָה תְּהִלָּה וְתִפְאֶרֶת קְדֻשָּׁה וּמַלְכוּת. בְּרָכוֹת
וְהוֹדָאוֹת מֵעַתָּה וְעַד עוֹלָם:

יְהַלְלוּךָ יְיָ אֱלֹהֵינוּ (עַל) כָּל מַעֲשֶׂיךָ וַחֲסִידֶיךָ צַדִּיקִים עוֹשֵׂי
רְצוֹנֶךָ וְכָל עַמְּךָ בֵּית יִשְׂרָאֵל בְּרִנָּה יוֹדוּ וִיבָרְכוּ
וִישַׁבְּחוּ וִיפָאֲרוּ וִירוֹמְמוּ וְיַעֲרִיצוּ וְיַקְדִּישׁוּ וְיַמְלִיכוּ אֶת שִׁמְךָ מַלְכֵּנוּ. כִּי לְךָ טוֹב
לְהוֹדוֹת וּלְשִׁמְךָ נָאֶה לְזַמֵּר כִּי מֵעוֹלָם וְעַד עוֹלָם אַתָּה אֵל: בָּרוּךְ אַתָּה יְיָ מֶלֶךְ
מְהֻלָּל בַּתִּשְׁבָּחוֹת:

הִנְנִי מוּכָן וּמְזֻמָּן לְקַיֵּם מִצְוַת כּוֹס רְבִיעִי שֶׁל אַרְבַּע כּוֹסוֹת לְשֵׁם יִחוּד קֻדְשָׁא בְּרִיךְ הוּא וּשְׁכִינְתֵּיהּ עַל יְדֵי הַהוּא טָמִיר וְנֶעְלָם
בְּשֵׁם כָּל יִשְׂרָאֵל:

בָּרוּךְ אַתָּה יְיָ אֱלֹהֵינוּ מֶלֶךְ הָעוֹלָם בּוֹרֵא פְּרִי הַגָּפֶן:

מֵסֵב וְשׁוֹתֶה הַכּוֹס, וּמְבָרֵךְ בְּרָכָה אַחֲרוֹנָה-אַחְכָא אֵין לִשְׁתּוֹתָיו.

בָּרוּךְ אַתָּה יְיָ אֱלֹהֵינוּ מֶלֶךְ הָעוֹלָם עַל הַגֶּפֶן וְעַל פְּרִי הַגֶּפֶן וְעַל אֶרֶץ חֶמְדָּה טוֹבָה וּרְחָבָה שֶׁרָצִיתָ
וְהִנְחַלְתָּ לַאֲבוֹתֵינוּ לֶאֱכֹל מִפִּרְיָהּ וְלִשְׂבּוֹעַ מִטּוּבָהּ. רַחֵם (נָא) יְיָ אֱלֹהֵינוּ עַל יִשְׂרָאֵל עַמֶּךָ וְעַל
יְרוּשָׁלַיִם עִירֶךָ וְעַל צִיּוֹן מִשְׁכַּן כְּבוֹדֶךָ וְעַל מִזְבְּחֶךָ וְעַל הֵיכָלֶךָ. וּבְנֵה יְרוּשָׁלַיִם עִיר הַקֹּדֶשׁ בִּמְהֵרָה בְיָמֵינוּ
וְהַעֲלֵנוּ לְתוֹכָהּ, וְשַׂמְּחֵנוּ בְּבִנְיָנָהּ. וְנֹאכַל מִפִּרְיָהּ. וְנִשְׂבַּע מִטּוּבָהּ. וּבְּרֶכְךָ עָלֶיהָ בִּקְדֻשָּׁה וּבְטָהֳרָה (בְּשַׁבָּת
וּרְצֵה וְהַחֲלִיצֵנוּ בְּיוֹם הַשַּׁבָּת הַזֶּה) וְשַׂמְּחֵנוּ בְּיוֹם חַג הַמַּצּוֹת הַזֶּה . כִּי אַתָּה יְיָ טוֹב וּמֵטִיב לַכֹּל וְנוֹדֶה לְךָ
עַל הָאָרֶץ וְעַל פְּרִי הַגָּפֶן: בָּרוּךְ אַתָּה יְיָ עַל הָאָרֶץ וְעַל פְּרִי הַגָּפֶן:

הַמְקַיֵּם מִצְוַת פֶּסַח כְּהִלְכָתָהּ, לְעַד עוֹמֶדֶת צִדְקָתוֹ.

נִרְצָה

Lord our God, all your works shall praise you. With song, the pious and the righteous who observe your will, and all of your people, the House of Israel, will acknowledge, bless, praise, glorify, exalt, extol, sanctify, and enthrone your Name, O our king. It is good to offer praise unto you, and it is proper to sing of your Name, since from everlasting to everlasting, you are God. Blessed are you, Lord, the king who is lauded with [songs of] praise.

The blessing over the fourth cup of wine is now recited.

Blessed are you, Lord our God, Sovereign of the Universe, who creates the fruit of the vine.

Barukh atah Adonai, Eloheinoo melekh ha-oh-lahm, boh-rei p'ree ha-gah-fen.

One reclines to the left, drinks the wine after the blessing, and afterwards refrains from drinking additional wine that night.

Blessed are you, Lord our God, King of the Universe, for the vine and for the fruit of the vine; and, for the fair, goodly, expansive land which you cherished, but still gave to our ancestors as an inheritance, so that we might eat of its fruit and enjoy its bounty. Kindly have mercy, Lord our God, upon Israel your people, upon Jerusalem your city, upon Zion the dwelling-place of your Glory, and, upon your altar and your Temple. Build the holy city of Jerusalem quickly, in our times. Bring us up to it so that we might rejoice in its rebuilding, eat of its fruit, enjoy its goodness, and bless you for it in sanctity and purity. (**On Sabbath, add:** May you strengthen us on this Sabbath day.) And, may you cause us to rejoice on this Festival of the *Matzot.* Because you, Lord, are good and benevolent to all, we thank you for the land and for the fruit of the vine. Blessed are you, Lord, for the land and for the fruit of the vine.

סֵדֶר פֶּסַח כְּהִלְכָתוֹ. כְּכָל מִשְׁפָּטוֹ וְחֻקָתוֹ. כַּאֲשֶׁר
זָכִינוּ לְסַדֵּר אוֹתוֹ. כֵּן נִזְכֶּה לַעֲשׂוֹתוֹ: זָךְ שׁוֹכֵן מְעוֹנָה
קוֹמֵם קְהַל עֲדַת מִי מָנָה. בְּקָרוֹב נַהֵל נִטְעֵי כַנָּה. פְּדוּיִם
לְצִיּוֹן בְּרִנָּה:

חֲסַל סִדּוּר פֶּסַח

לְשָׁנָה הַבָּאָה בִּירוּשָׁלָיִם

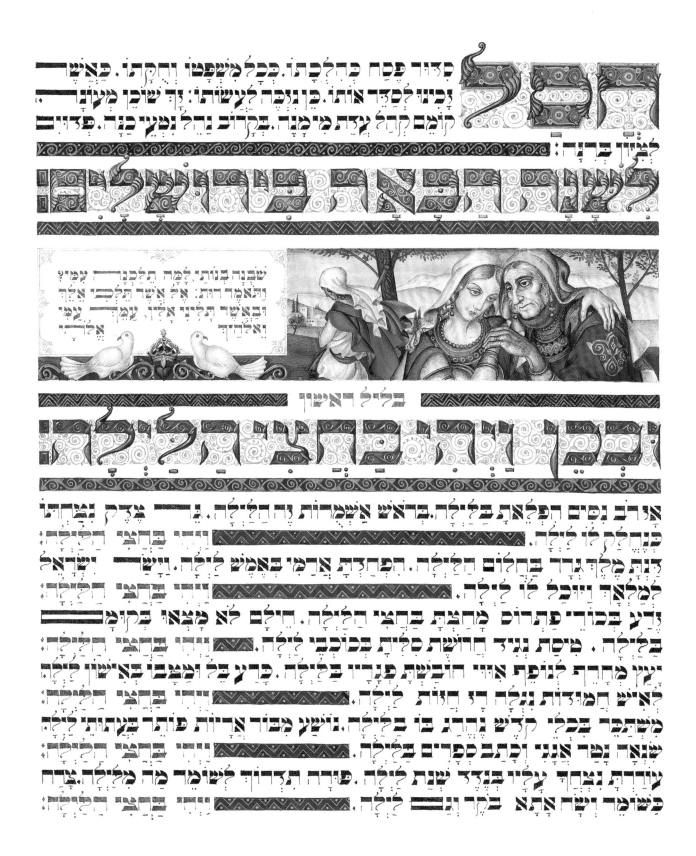

שׁוּבָה כְּנוֹתַי לָמָה תֵלַכְנָה עִמִּי?
וַתֹּאמַרְנָה: אֶל אֲשֶׁר תֵּלְכִי אֵלֵךְ
וּבַאֲשֶׁר תָּלִינִי אָלִין, עַמֵּךְ,
וֵאלֹהַיִךְ...

בליל ראשון

וּבְכֵן וַיְהִי בַּחֲצִי הַלַּיְלָה

אָז רוֹב נִסִּים הִפְלֵאתָ בַּלַּיְלָה. בְּרֹאשׁ אַשְׁמוֹרוֹת זֶה הַלַּיְלָה. גֵּר צֶדֶק נִצַּחְתּוֹ
כְּנֶחֱלַק לוֹ לַיְלָה. וַיְהִי בַּחֲצִי הַלַּיְלָה.

דַּנְתָּ מֶלֶךְ גְּרָר בַּחֲלוֹם הַלַּיְלָה. הִפְחַדְתָּ אֲרַמִּי בְּאֶמֶשׁ לַיְלָה. וַיָּשַׂר יִשְׂרָאֵל
לְמַלְאָךְ וַיּוּכַל לוֹ לַיְלָה. וַיְהִי בַּחֲצִי הַלַּיְלָה.

זֶרַע בְּכוֹרֵי פַתְרוֹס מָחַצְתָּ בַּחֲצִי הַלַּיְלָה. חֵילָם לֹא מָצְאוּ בְּקוּמָם
בַּלַּיְלָה. טִיסַת נְגִיד חֲרֹשֶׁת סִלִּיתָ בְּכוֹכְבֵי לַיְלָה. וַיְהִי בַּחֲצִי לַיְלָה.

יָעַץ מְחָרֵף לְנוֹפֵף אִוּוּי הוֹבַשְׁתָּ פְגָרָיו בַּלַּיְלָה. כָּרַע בֵּל וּמַצָּבוֹ בְּאִישׁוֹן
לַיְלָה. לְאִישׁ חֲמוּדוֹת נִגְלָה רָז חֲזוֹת לַיְלָה. וַיְהִי בַּחֲצִי לַיְלָה.

מִשְׁתַּכֵּר בִּכְלֵי קֹדֶשׁ נֶהֱרַג בּוֹ בַלַּיְלָה. נוֹשַׁע מִבּוֹר אֲרָיוֹת פּוֹתֵר בִּעֲתוּתֵי לַיְלָה.
שִׂנְאָה נָטַר אֲגָגִי וְכָתַב סְפָרִים בַּלַּיְלָה. וַיְהִי בַּחֲצִי לַיְלָה.

עוֹרַרְתָּ נִצְחֲךָ עָלָיו בְּנֶדֶד שְׁנַת לַיְלָה. פּוּרָה תִדְרוֹךְ לְשׁוֹמֵר מַה מִלַּיְלָה. צָרַח
כַּשּׁוֹמֵר וְשָׂח אָתָא בֹקֶר וְגַם לַיְלָה. וַיְהִי בַּחֲצִי לַיְלָה.

"Who celebrates the feast aright, acquires grace in heaven's sight."

NEERTZAH: May Our Service Be Accepted

Neertzah, the fifteenth part, formally concludes the Seder. Though the Exodus celebrated on Passover is the paradigmatic redemptive event in Jewish history, tradition views it as a penultimate prelude to the final messianic redemption—a time when all oppression and war will end, and justice and peace will prevail. This is the sentiment reflected in the concluding hymn of *Neertzah*, which is drawn from a longer hymn by the eleventh-century liturgical poet Joseph Tov Elem. It is customarily recited by Ashkenazic Jews. As in much of Jewish religious literature, the final redemption is closely linked to the restoration of Jewish sovereignty over the Land of Israel and the rebuilding of the Temple. It is not surprising, therefore, that after this hymn, the phrase "Next year in Jerusalem" is added. See Commentary, pages 33–37.

The Passover Seder has now been properly concluded, according to all its laws and statutes. Just as we have been worthy to celebrate it, so have we been privileged to observe it. O Pure One, who dwells on high, raise up the fecund flock [of Israel]. With song, speedily lead to Zion the shoots of your stock—redeemed!

NEXT YEAR IN JERUSALEM!

Here some sing "Next Year in Jerusalem" in Hebrew: L'shanah ha-bah-ah b'y'rooshah-lah-yeem.

THE HYMNS AND SONGS

Hymns (*piyyutim*) and songs (*zemirot*) constitute a medieval addendum to the formal structure of the fifteen parts of the Seder, thereby concluding the Seder with hope, joy and song. This first hymn is based on a tradition that major redemptive events in biblical history, from Abraham to Esther, occurred at night, specifically on the night of Passover. This hymn ends with a plea for the dawning of the messianic era—a time in which the redemptive light of day will eclipse the long night of darkness, exile, injustice, and oppression. Excerpts from these hymns follow in translation. On oppression and redemption, see Commentary, pages 33–36.

"VAH-Y'HEE BA-ḤATZEE HA-LY-LAH" ("In the Middle of the Night, It Came to Pass")
(first night only)

You meted out justice to the king of Gerar in a dream of the night (Genesis 20). You struck terror into Laban in the darkness of the night (Genesis 31). Israel wrestled with an angel and prevailed at night (Genesis 32). *In the middle of the night, it came to pass.* [. . .]

Belshazzar, the drunken ruler of Babylonia was murdered during the night (Daniel 5). Saved from the lion's den, Daniel interpreted dreams at night. Hateful Haman wrote his [evil] decrees at night. *In the middle of the night, it came to pass.*

קֶרֶב יוֹם אֲשֶׁר הוּא לֹא יוֹם וְלֹא לַיְלָה. רָם הוֹדַע כִּי לְךָ הַיּוֹם אַף לְךָ
לַיְלָה. שׁוֹמְרִים הַפְקֵד לְעִירְךָ כָּל הַיּוֹם וְכָל הַלַּיְלָה. תָּאִיר כְּאוֹר יוֹם
חֶשְׁכַּת לַיְלָה: וַיְהִי בַּחֲצִי הַלָּיְלָה:

בְּלֵיל שִׁמֻּרִים

אֹמֶץ גְּבוּרוֹתֶיךָ הִפְלֵאתָ בַּפֶּסַח. בְּרֹאשׁ כָּל
מוֹעֲדוֹת נִשֵּׂאתָ פֶּסַח. גִּלִּיתָ לָאֱזְרָחִי חֲצוֹת לֵיל
פֶּסַח. וַאֲמַרְתֶּם זֶבַח פֶּסַח.

דְּלָתָיו דָּפַקְתָּ כְּחֹם הַיּוֹם בַּפֶּסַח. הִסְעִיד נוֹצְצִים
עֻגוֹת מַצּוֹת בַּפֶּסַח. וְאֶל הַבָּקָר רָץ זֵכֶר לְשׁוֹר
עֵרֶךְ פֶּסַח. וַאֲמַרְתֶּם זֶבַח פֶּסַח.

זוֹעֲמוּ סְדוֹמִים וְלוֹהֲטוּ בָּאֵשׁ בַּפֶּסַח. חֻלַּץ לוֹט
מֵהֶם וּמַצּוֹת אָפָה בְּקֵץ פֶּסַח. טִאטֵאתָ אַדְמַת
מוֹף וְנוֹף בְּעָבְרְךָ בַּפֶּסַח. וַאֲמַרְתֶּם זֶבַח פֶּסַח.

יָהּ רֹאשׁ כָּל אוֹן מָחַצְתָּ בְּלֵיל שִׁמּוּר פֶּסַח.
כַּבִּיר עַל בֵּן בְּכוֹר פָּסַחְתָּ בְּדַם פֶּסַח. לְבִלְתִּי
תֵּת מַשְׁחִית לָבֹא בִּפְתָחַי בַּפֶּסַח. וַאֲמַרְתֶּם זֶבַח פֶּסַח.

מְסֻגֶּרֶת סֻגָּרָה בְּעִתּוֹתֵי פֶּסַח. נִשְׁמְדָה מִדְיָן בִּצְלִיל שְׂעוֹרֵי עֹמֶר פֶּסַח. שׂוֹרְפוּ
מִשְׁמַנֵּי פּוּל וְלוּד בִּיקַד יְקוֹד פֶּסַח. וַאֲמַרְתֶּם זֶבַח פֶּסַח.

עוֹד הַיּוֹם בְּנֹב לַעֲמוֹד עַד גָּעָה עוֹנַת פֶּסַח. פַּס יַד כָּתְבָה לְקַעֲקֵעַ צוּל בַּפֶּסַח.
צָפֹה הַצָּפִית עָרוֹךְ הַשֻּׁלְחָן בַּפֶּסַח. וַאֲמַרְתֶּם זֶבַח פֶּסַח.

קָהָל כִּנְּסָה הֲדַסָּה צוֹם לְשַׁלֵּשׁ בַּפֶּסַח. רֹאשׁ מִבֵּית רָשָׁע מָחַצְתָּ בְּעֵץ חֲמִשִּׁים
בַּפֶּסַח. שְׁתֵּי אֵלֶּה רֶגַע תָּבִיא לְעוּצִית בַּפֶּסַח. תָּעֹז יָדְךָ וְתָרוּם יְמִינְךָ כְּלֵיל הִתְקַדֵּשׁ
חַג פֶּסַח. וַאֲמַרְתֶּם זֶבַח פֶּסַח.

Hasten the day that is [a continuous day,] neither day nor night (Zechariah 14:7). God on high, proclaim that yours is the day and also the night. Place watchmen to guard your city by day and by night. Make the darkness of the night [that is, the times of exile and oppression] as bright as the light of the day [that is, the light of redemptive times]. *And may this come to pass, in the middle of the night.*

"VA-AMARTEM ZEVAḤ PESAḤ" ("Thus, You Should Say—'This Is the Paschal Offering'")
(second night only)

A complex liturgical poem by Elazar ben Kallir (probably sixth-century), the greatest of the early liturgical poets, this hymn, like the preceding one, contains many obscure references to rabbinic interpretations of events narrated in the Bible. Also, like the previous hymn: it is in Hebrew alphabetic acrostic form; it recounts redemptive biblical events from Abraham to Esther that tradition identifies with the time of Passover; and, it concludes with the hope for the restoration of the Temple service on Passover in messianic times. See Commentary sections on *matzah* and the motif of redemption, pages 17, 34–35.

In the heat of the day, you visited Abraham on Passover. Abraham fed the visiting angels cakes of *matzah* on Passover, and ran to the herd to get a calf [to consume], to commemorate the Passover (Genesis 18). *Thus you should say, "This is the Paschal offering."* [. . .]

God, you smote the firstborn of the [idol-worshipping] cult [of Egypt] on the night of Passover. But, Mighty God, you passed over [and spared] the firstborn [of Israel] when you passed over [the houses whose lintels were smeared with] blood [of the sacrifice] of Passover. Nor did you permit the destroyer to enter the [marked] doors [of the Israelites] on Passover (Exodus 12). *Thus should you say, "This is the Paschal offering."* [. . .]

At Nob [on the outskirts of Jerusalem Sennacherib] paused [before attacking Jerusalem], but his arrogance brought about his suffering, on Passover (Isaiah 10:12). Upon the wall, a hand wrote [in the presence of Belshazzar, king of Babylonia] of the destruction [of Babylonia, and of its descent] into an abyss, on Passover (Daniel 5). "Let the watchman watch; set the table," [say the Babylonians on the eve of their destruction] (Isaiah 21:3–10), on Passover. *Thus you should say, "This is the Paschal offering."*

אַדִּיר בִּמְלוּכָה. בָּחוּר כַּהֲלָכָה. גְּדוּדָיו יֹאמְרוּ לוֹ. לְךָ וּלְךָ. לְךָ כִּי לְךָ. לְךָ אַף לְךָ. לְךָ יְיָ הַמַּמְלָכָה. כִּי לוֹ נָאֶה. כִּי לוֹ יָאֶה: דָּגוּל בִּמְלוּכָה. הָדוּר כַּהֲלָכָה. וָתִיקָיו יֹאמְרוּ לוֹ. לְךָ וּלְךָ. לְךָ כִּי לְךָ אַף לְךָ. לְךָ יְיָ הַמַּמְלָכָה. כִּי לוֹ נָאֶה. כִּי לוֹ יָאֶה. זַכַּאי בִּמְלוּכָה. חָסִין כַּהֲלָכָה מַפְסְרָיו יֹאמְרוּ לוֹ. לְךָ וּלְךָ. לְךָ כִּי לְךָ. לְךָ אַף לְךָ. לְךָ יְיָ הַמַּמְלָכָה. כִּי לוֹ נָאֶה. כִּי לוֹ יָאֶה. טַהוֹר בִּמְלוּכָה. יָחִיד בִּמְלוּכָה. כַּבִּיר כַּהֲלָכָה. לִמּוּדָיו יֹאמְרוּ לוֹ. לְךָ וּלְךָ. לְךָ כִּי לְךָ. לְךָ אַף לְךָ. לְךָ יְיָ הַמַּמְלָכָה. כִּי לוֹ נָאֶה. כִּי לוֹ יָאֶה: מוֹשֵׁל בִּמְלוּכָה. נוֹרָא כַּהֲלָכָה. סְבִיבָיו יֹאמְרוּ לוֹ. לְךָ וּלְךָ. לְךָ כִּי לְךָ. לְךָ אַף לְךָ. לְךָ יְיָ הַמַּמְלָכָה. כִּי לוֹ נָאֶה. כִּי לוֹ יָאֶה: עָנָו בִּמְלוּכָה. פּוֹדֶה כַּהֲלָכָה. צַדִּיקָיו יֹאמְרוּ לוֹ. לְךָ וּלְךָ. לְךָ כִּי לְךָ. לְךָ אַף לְךָ. לְךָ יְיָ הַמַּמְלָכָה. כִּי לוֹ נָאֶה. כִּי לוֹ יָאֶה: קָדוֹשׁ בִּמְלוּכָה. רַחוּם כַּהֲלָכָה. שִׁנְאַנָּיו יֹאמְרוּ לוֹ. לְךָ וּלְךָ. לְךָ כִּי לְךָ. לְךָ אַף לְךָ. לְךָ יְיָ הַמַּמְלָכָה. כִּי לוֹ נָאֶה. כִּי לוֹ יָאֶה: תַּקִּיף בִּמְלוּכָה. תּוֹמֵךְ כַּהֲלָכָה. תְּמִימָיו יֹאמְרוּ לוֹ. לְךָ וּלְךָ. לְךָ כִּי לְךָ. לְךָ אַף לְךָ. לְךָ יְיָ הַמַּמְלָכָה. כִּי לוֹ נָאֶה. כִּי לוֹ יָאֶה:

אַדִּיר הוּא. יִבְנֶה בֵיתוֹ בְּקָרוֹב. בִּמְהֵרָה בִּמְהֵרָה בְּיָמֵינוּ בְּקָרוֹב. אֵל בְּנֵה. אֵל בְּנֵה. בְּנֵה בֵיתְךָ בְּקָרוֹב: בָּחוּר הוּא. גָּדוֹל הוּא. דָּגוּל הוּא. יִבְנֶה בֵיתוֹ בְּקָרוֹב בִּמְהֵרָה בִּמְהֵרָה בְּיָמֵינוּ בְּקָרוֹב. אֵל: הָדוּר הוּא. וָתִיק הוּא. זַכַּאי הוּא. חָסִיד הוּא. יִבְנֶה בֵיתוֹ בְּקָרוֹב. בִּמְהֵרָה בִּמְהֵרָה בְּיָמֵינוּ בְּקָרוֹב. אֵל: טָהוֹר הוּא יָחִיד הוּא. כַּבִּיר הוּא. לָמוּד הוּא. מֶלֶךְ הוּא. נוֹרָא הוּא. סַגִּיב הוּא. עִזּוּז הוּא. פּוֹדֶה הוּא. צַדִּיק הוּא. יִבְנֶה בֵיתוֹ בְּקָרוֹב. בִּמְהֵרָה בִּמְהֵרָה בְּיָמֵינוּ בְּקָרוֹב. אֵל: קָדוֹשׁ הוּא. רַחוּם הוּא. שַׁדַּי הוּא. תַּקִּיף הוּא. יִבְנֶה בֵיתוֹ בְּקָרוֹב. בִּמְהֵרָה בִּמְהֵרָה בְּיָמֵינוּ בְּקָרוֹב. אֵל בְּנֵה. אֵל בְּנֵה. בְּנֵה בֵיתְךָ בְּקָרוֹב:

These two popular hymns—"Kee Loh Nah-Eh" ("Yours, Only Yours") and "Adeer Hoo" are often sung consecutively with great enthusiasm. Both are in Hebrew alphabetical acrostic form. Their authors are unknown. Though neither hymn was specifically composed for Passover, the first began to appear in haggadot in the thirteenth century, and the second in the fourteenth century. The first expresses praise of God's attributes, such as power, love, and wisdom. The second expresses praise of God's attributes and calls for the onset of imminent messianic redemption with God's rebuilding of the Holy Temple in Jerusalem. The first is left untranslated, while the second is both translated and transliterated.

"ADEER HOO" ("Mighty Is He")
(both nights)

Repeat this refrain after each stanza:

He will build his Temple soon: speedily, speedily; in our days and soon. God—build, God—build. Build your Temple, and do it soon!

Yeev-neh veitoh b'kah-rohv, beem-hei-rah, beem-hei-rah. B'yah-mei-noo b'kah-rohv. Eil b'nei. Eil b'nei. B'nei vei-t'khah b'kah-rohv.

1. **Mighty is he, mighty is he.**
2. **Chosen is he, great is he, preeminent is he, glorious is he, ancient is he, worthy is he, pious is he.**
3. **Pure is he, unique is he, powerful is he, learned is he, a king is he, awesome is he, stupendous is he, strong is he, a redeemer is he, righteous is he.**
4. **Holy is he, compassionate is he, omnipotent is he, powerful is he.**

1. Adeer hoo, adeer hoo.
2. Baḥoor hoo, gah-dohl hoo, dah-gool hoo. Ha-door hoo, vah-teek hoo, zah-kai hoo, ḥah-seed hoo.
3. Tah-hohr hoo, yah-ḥeed hoo, kah-beer hoo, lah-mood hoo, melekh hoo, noh-rah hoo, sah-geev hoo, ee-zooz hoo, poh-deh hoo, tzah-deek hoo.
4. Kah-dosh hoo, rah-ḥoom hoo, shah-dy hoo, tah-keef hoo.

NOTE: Though not found in *The Szyk Haggadah*, it is customary to begin counting the "*omeir*" here; see Commentary, page 48.

מִי יוֹדֵעַ. אֶחָד אֲנִי יוֹדֵעַ. אֶחָד אֱלֹהֵינוּ שֶׁבַּשָּׁמַיִם וּבָאָרֶץ:

אֱלֹהֵינוּ שֶׁבַּשָּׁמַיִם וּבָאָרֶץ:

מִי יוֹדֵעַ. שְׁלֹשָׁה אֲנִי יוֹדֵעַ. שְׁלֹשָׁה אָבוֹת. שְׁנֵי לוּחוֹת הַבְּרִית. אֶחָד אֱלֹהֵינוּ שֶׁבַּשָּׁמַיִם וּבָאָרֶץ:

מִי יוֹדֵעַ. אַרְבַּע אֲנִי יוֹדֵעַ. אַרְבַּע אִמָּהוֹת. שְׁלֹשָׁה אָבוֹת. שְׁנֵי לוּחוֹת הַבְּרִית. אֶחָד אֱלֹהֵינוּ שֶׁבַּשָּׁמַיִם וּבָאָרֶץ:

מִי יוֹדֵעַ. חֲמִשָּׁה אֲנִי יוֹדֵעַ. חֲמִשָּׁה חוּמְשֵׁי תוֹרָה. אַרְבַּע אִמָּהוֹת. שְׁלֹשָׁה אָבוֹת. שְׁנֵי לוּחוֹת הַבְּרִית. אֶחָד אֱלֹהֵינוּ שֶׁבַּשָּׁמַיִם וּבָאָרֶץ:

מִי יוֹדֵעַ. שִׁשָּׁה אֲנִי יוֹדֵעַ. שִׁשָּׁה סִדְרֵי מִשְׁנָה. חֲמִשָּׁה חוּמְשֵׁי תוֹרָה. אַרְבַּע אִמָּהוֹת. שְׁלֹשָׁה אָבוֹת. שְׁנֵי לוּחוֹת הַבְּרִית. אֶחָד אֱלֹהֵינוּ שֶׁבַּשָּׁמַיִם וּבָאָרֶץ:

מִי יוֹדֵעַ. שִׁבְעָה אֲנִי יוֹדֵעַ. שִׁבְעָה יְמֵי שַׁבַּתָּא. שִׁשָּׁה סִדְרֵי מִשְׁנָה. חֲמִשָּׁה חוּמְשֵׁי תוֹרָה. אַרְבַּע אִמָּהוֹת. שְׁלֹשָׁה אָבוֹת. שְׁנֵי לוּחוֹת הַבְּרִית. אֶחָד אֱלֹהֵינוּ שֶׁבַּשָּׁמַיִם וּבָאָרֶץ:

מִי יוֹדֵעַ. שְׁמוֹנָה אֲנִי יוֹדֵעַ. שְׁמוֹנָה יְמֵי מִילָה. שִׁבְעָה יְמֵי שַׁבַּתָּא. שִׁשָּׁה סִדְרֵי מִשְׁנָה. חֲמִשָּׁה חוּמְשֵׁי תוֹרָה. אַרְבַּע אִמָּהוֹת. שְׁלֹשָׁה אָבוֹת. שְׁנֵי לוּחוֹת הַבְּרִית. אֶחָד אֱלֹהֵינוּ שֶׁבַּשָּׁמַיִם וּבָאָרֶץ:

מִי יוֹדֵעַ. תִּשְׁעָה אֲנִי יוֹדֵעַ. תִּשְׁעָה יַרְחֵי לֵדָה. שְׁמוֹנָה יְמֵי מִילָה. שִׁבְעָה יְמֵי שַׁבַּתָּא. שִׁשָּׁה סִדְרֵי מִשְׁנָה. חֲמִשָּׁה חוּמְשֵׁי תוֹרָה. אַרְבַּע אִמָּהוֹת. שְׁלֹשָׁה אָבוֹת. שְׁנֵי לוּחוֹת הַבְּרִית. אֶחָד אֱלֹהֵינוּ שֶׁבַּשָּׁמַיִם וּבָאָרֶץ:

מִי יוֹדֵעַ. עֲשָׂרָה אֲנִי יוֹדֵעַ. עֲשָׂרָה דִבְּרַיָּא. תִּשְׁעָה יַרְחֵי לֵדָה. שְׁמוֹנָה יְמֵי מִילָה. שִׁבְעָה יְמֵי שַׁבַּתָּא. שִׁשָּׁה סִדְרֵי מִשְׁנָה. חֲמִשָּׁה חוּמְשֵׁי תוֹרָה. אַרְבַּע אִמָּהוֹת. שְׁלֹשָׁה אָבוֹת. שְׁנֵי לוּחוֹת הַבְּרִית. אֶחָד אֱלֹהֵינוּ שֶׁבַּשָּׁמַיִם וּבָאָרֶץ:

"EHAD MEE YOH-DEI-AH" ("Who Knows One?")
(both nights)

The author of this popular song is unknown. It may have been composed as early as the fourteenth century, and is first found in printed form in the famous 1590 *Prague Haggadah*. The song, composed in the form of question-and-answer, in Hebrew and Aramaic, is pedagogic in nature and aims at engaging the interest and participation of the children at the Seder. The popular tune to which it is sung is reminiscent of sixteenth-century German folk songs. This page translates and explains references in the song; see the next page for a transliteration.

Ask a different person to sing the answer to each question. As the song builds, each person gives his or her answer in turn from one to thirteen.

ONE, *who knows* [what it represents]?
ONE, *I know.*
ONE *is our God who is in heaven and earth.*

TWO, *who knows?*
TWO, *I know.*
TWO *are the Tablets.*
ONE *is our God who is in heaven and earth.*

THREE: the Patriarchs.
FOUR: the Matriarchs.
FIVE: the Books of the Torah.
SIX: the "orders" of the Mishnah.
SEVEN: the days of the week.
EIGHT: the days to circumcision.
NINE: the months of pregnancy.
TEN: the Commandments.
ELEVEN: the stars in Joseph's dream.
TWELVE: the tribes of Israel.
THIRTEEN: the attributes of God.

EXPLANATION: *One* refers to the monotheistic belief in one God who created all that exists. *Two* refers to the two tablets that Moses brought down from Mount Sinai. *Three* refers to: Abraham, Isaac, and Jacob. *Four* refers to: Sarah, Rebecca, Rachel, and Leah. *Five* refers to: Genesis, Exodus, Leviticus, Numbers, and Deuteronomy. *Six* refers to the six "orders" (or sections) of the Mishnah that were codified in the third century by Rabbi Judah the Prince: "Seeds" (agricultural laws), "Appointed Seasons" (laws of the Sabbath and festivals), "Women" (marriage, divorce, etc.), "Damages" (torts, commercial law, jurisprudence), "Sanctities" (sacrifices), "Purification" (ritual contamination and purification). *Seven* refers to the days of the week; though in the secular calendar the days of the week have names (e.g., Monday), in the Jewish calendar, except for the Sabbath (Shabbat), days have no names, only numbers, e.g., "Day One" (Sunday), "Day Two" (Monday). *Eight* refers to the number of days from the birth of a boy to his circumcision. *Nine* are the months of human gestation. *Ten* refers to the Ten Commandments (Exodus 20:1–14, Deuteronomy 5:6–18). *Eleven* refers to the stars in Joseph's dream (Genesis 37:9), representing his brothers. *Twelve* are the twelve tribes of Israel. *Thirteen* refers to God's attributes, as given in Exodus 34:6–7.

מי יודע אחד עשר. אני יודע. אחד עשר
כוכביא. עשרה דבריא. תשעה ירחי לדה.
שמונה ימי מילה. שבעה ימי שבתא. ששה
סדרי משנה. חמשה חומשי תורה.
ארבע אמהות. שלשה אבות. שני
לוחות הברית. אחד אלד
שבשמים ובארץ:

מי יודע אחד עשר. אני יודע. אחד עשר
כוכביא. עשרה דבריא. תשעה ירחי לדה.
שבטיא. אחד עשר כוכביא. עשרה
דבריא. תשעה ירחי לדה. שמונה
ימי מילה. שבעה ימי שבתא. ששה סדרי
משנה. חמשה חומשי תורה. ארבע אמהות.
שלשה אבות. שני לוחות הברית. אחד
אלהינו שבשמים ובארץ:

החזק חנית וסגר לקראת רדפי אמר לנפשי ישעתך אני:

"EḤAD MEE YOH-DEI-AH" ("Who Knows One?")

This song is sung according to the following formula:
[Number 1–13] *mee yoh-dei-ah?*
[Number 1–13] *ah-nee yoh-dei-ah.*
[Number 1–13] [what that number represents, given in the list below in italics after the colon]

Then the previous numbers and their meanings are recounted, ending with the refrain. Begin with numbers 1 and 2, written out below:

   1. Eḥad *mee yoh-dei-ah?*
      Eḥad *ah-nee yoh-dei-ah.*

      Refrain: Eḥad *Eloheinoo, Eloheinoo, Eloheinoo, sheh-bah-shah-mah-yeem oo-vah-ah-retz.*

   2. Sh'nah-yeem *mee yoh-dei-ah?*
      Sh'nah-yeem *ah-nee yoh-dei-ah.*
      Sh'nai *loo-ḥoht ha-breet.*

      Refrain: Eḥad *Eloheinoo, Eloheinoo, Eloheinoo, sheh-bah-shah-mah-yeem oo-vah-ah-retz.*

   3. Sheh-loh-shah: *ah-voht.*
   4. Ahr-bah: *eemah-hoht.*
   5. Ḥamee-shah: *ḥoom-shei Torah.*
   6. Shee-shah: *seed-rei meesh-nah.*
   7. Shee-vah: *y'mei shah-ba-ta.*
   8. Sh'moh-nah: *y'mei mee-lah.*
   9. Tee-sha: *yar-ḥei lei-dah.*
 10. Asah-rah: *deeb-ry-yah.*
 11. Eḥad asar: *kokh-vah-yah.*
 12. Sh'naim-asar: *sheev-ty-yah.*
 13. Sh'losh-ah asar: *meed-ah-yah.*

חַד גַּדְיָא

דְּזַבִּין אַבָּא בִּתְרֵי זוּזֵי. חַד גַּדְיָא. חַד גַּדְיָא: וְאָתָא שׁוּנְרָא. וְאָכְלָה לְגַדְיָא. דְּזַבִּין אַבָּא בִּתְרֵי זוּזֵי. חַד גַּדְיָא.
חַד גַּדְיָא: וְאָתָא כַלְבָּא. וְנָשַׁךְ לְשׁוּנְרָא. דְּאָכְלָה לְגַדְיָא. דְּזַבִּין אַבָּא בִּתְרֵי זוּזֵי. חַד גַּדְיָא. חַד גַּדְיָא: וְאָתָא
חוּטְרָא. וְהִכָּה לְכַלְבָּא. דְּנָשַׁךְ לְשׁוּנְרָא. דְּאָכְלָה לְגַדְיָא. דְּזַבִּין אַבָּא בִּתְרֵי זוּזֵי. חַד גַּדְיָא. חַד גַּדְיָא: וְאָתָא
נוּרָא. וְשָׂרַף לְחוּטְרָא. דְּהִכָּה לְכַלְבָּא. דְּנָשַׁךְ לְשׁוּנְרָא. דְּאָכְלָה לְגַדְיָא. דְּזַבִּין אַבָּא בִּתְרֵי זוּזֵי. חַד גַּדְיָא. חַד גַּדְיָא: וְאָתָא
מַיָּא. וְכָבָה לְנוּרָא. דְּשָׂרַף לְחוּטְרָא. דְּהִכָּה לְכַלְבָּא. דְּנָשַׁךְ לְשׁוּנְרָא. דְּאָכְלָה לְגַדְיָא. דְּזַבִּין אַבָּא בִּתְרֵי זוּזֵי. חַד
גַּדְיָא. חַד גַּדְיָא: וְאָתָא תוֹרָא. וְשָׁתָה לְמַיָּא. דְּכָבָה לְנוּרָא. דְּשָׂרַף לְחוּטְרָא. דְּהִכָּה לְכַלְבָּא. דְּנָשַׁךְ לְשׁוּנְרָא.
דְּאָכְלָה לְגַדְיָא. דְּזַבִּין אַבָּא בִּתְרֵי זוּזֵי. חַד גַּדְיָא. חַד גַּדְיָא: וְאָתָא הַשּׁוֹחֵט. וְשָׁחַט לְתוֹרָא. דְּשָׁתָה לְמַיָּא.
דְּכָבָה לְנוּרָא. דְּשָׂרַף לְחוּטְרָא. דְּהִכָּה לְכַלְבָּא. דְּנָשַׁךְ לְשׁוּנְרָא. דְּאָכְלָה לְגַדְיָא. דְּזַבִּין אַבָּא בִּתְרֵי זוּזֵי.
חַד גַּדְיָא. חַד גַּדְיָא: וְאָתָא מַלְאַךְ הַמָּוֶת. וְשָׁחַט לְשׁוֹחֵט. דְּשָׁחַט לְתוֹרָא. דְּשָׁתָה לְמַיָּא. דְּכָבָה לְנוּרָא.
דְּשָׂרַף לְחוּטְרָא. דְּהִכָּה לְכַלְבָּא. דְּנָשַׁךְ לְשׁוּנְרָא. דְּאָכְלָה לְגַדְיָא. דְּזַבִּין אַבָּא בִּתְרֵי זוּזֵי. חַד גַּדְיָא. חַד גַּ
חַד גַּדְיָא: וְאָתָא הַקָּדוֹשׁ בָּרוּךְ הוּא. וְשָׁחַט לְמַלְאַךְ הַמָּוֶת. דְּשָׁחַט לְשׁוֹחֵט. דְּשָׁחַט לְתוֹרָא. דְּשָׁתָא
לְמַיָּא. דְּכָבָה לְנוּרָא. דְּשָׂרַף לְחוּטְרָא. דְּהִכָּה לְכַלְבָּא. דְּנָשַׁךְ לְשׁוּנְרָא. דְּאָכְלָה לְגַדְיָא. דְּזַבִּין אַבָּא
בִּתְרֵי זוּזֵי. חַד גַּדְיָא. חַד גַּדְיָא:

פֶּסַח

"ḤAD GADYA" ("One Kid")
(both nights)

Like the preceding song ("Who Knows One?") the following popular song, "Ḥad Gadya," appeared in printed form for the first time in the 1590 *Prague Haggadah*, and its author is unknown. On the motif of retribution, see Commentary, pages 40–42.

Someone may be designated to sing the stanzas, while all can respond with the
refrain:

> D'zah-been abba bee-trei zoozei, ḥad gadya, ḥad gadya.

Some add sounds while they are singing representing the "characters" in the song,
"meow" for the cat, "bow-wow" for the dog, etc.

The one kid, the one kid, that Daddy bought for two *zoozeem*: the one kid, the one kid.

Then came the cat and ate the kid, that Daddy bought for two *zoozeem*: the one kid, the one kid.

Then came the dog that bit the cat that ate the kid, that Daddy bought for two *zoozeem*: the one kid, the one kid.

Then came the stick that struck the dog that bit the cat that ate the kid, that Daddy bought for two *zoozeem*: the one kid, the one kid.

Then came the fire that burned the stick that struck the dog that bit the cat that ate the kid, that Daddy bought for two *zoozeem*: the one kid, the one kid.

Then came the water that quenched the fire that burned the stick that struck the dog that bit the cat that ate the kid, that Daddy bought for two *zoozeem*: the one kid, the one kid.

Then came the ox that drank the water that quenched the fire that burned the stick that struck the dog that bit the cat that ate the kid, that Daddy bought for two *zoozeem*: the one kid, the one kid.

Then came the butcher who butchered the ox that drank the water that quenched the fire that burned the stick that struck the dog that bit the cat that ate the kid, that Daddy bought for two *zoozeem*: the one kid, the one kid.

Then came the Angel of Death who butchered the butcher who butchered the ox that drank the water that quenched the fire that burned the stick that struck the dog that bit the cat that ate the kid, that Daddy bought for two *zoozeem*: the one kid, the one kid.

And then came the Blessed Holy One who slaughtered the Angel of Death who butchered the butcher who butchered the ox that drank the water that quenched the fire that burned the stick that struck the dog that bit the cat that ate the kid, that Daddy bought for two *zoozeem*: the one kid, the one kid.

Arthur Szyk concludes his Haggadah with a citation from Psalms and a phrase traditionally recited at the end of the yearly cycle of reading the Torah. On the tablet held by King David, traditionally considered the author of the psalms, a verse from Psalms expresses the hope that the deliverance of Israel—celebrated at the Seder—will have its roots in Zion, in the restored Land of Israel. The final phrase suggests that such deliverance will only come through strength—physical and spiritual. For Szyk and Zionism, see Commentary, pages 36–37.

O that the deliverance of Israel may come from Zion! When the Lord restores the fortunes of his people, Jacob will rejoice, Israel will be glad (Psalms 14:7).

Ḥazak! Ḥazak! V'neet-ḥazeik!—
"Be strong! Be strong! And, let us be strengthened!"

THE HAGGADAH

COMMENTARY

BYRON L. SHERWIN *with* IRVIN UNGAR

A HISTORICANA BOOK

ABRAMS, NEW YORK

I am but a Jew praying in art.
If I have succeeded in any measure,
if I have gained the power of reception
among the elite of the world,
then I owe it all
to the teachings, traditions, and
eternal virtues of my people.

ARTHUR SZYK
Imagier of Israel

"If I forget you, O Jerusalem, let my right hand wither."
(Psalms 137:5)

JE NE SUIS QU'UN JUIF EN PRIÈRE D'ART
ET SI J'AI TRAVAILLÉ, SI DANS QUELQUE
MESURE J'AI RÉUSSI, SI J'AI TROUVÉ
ACCUEIL DE FAVEUR DANS L'ÉLITE DU
MONDE, JE LE DOIS AUX ENSEIGNEMENTS,
AUX TRADITIONS, AUX VERTUS
ÉTERNELLES DE MA RACE.....

Editor: Aiah Rachel Wieder
Designer: Darilyn Lowe Carnes
Art Direction: Michelle Ishay
Production Manager: Anet Sirna-Bruder

Library of Congress Cataloging-in-Publication Data

Haggadah. English & Hebrew.
The Szyk Haggadah / Arthur Szyk ; translation and commentary by Byron L. Sherwin with Irvin Ungar.
    p. cm.
ISBN 978-0-8109-9745-5 (hardcover : alk. paper)—ISBN 978-0-8109-9753-0
(pbk. : alk. paper)
1. Haggadot—Texts. 2. Seder—Liturgy—Texts.
3. Judaism—Liturgy—Texts. 4. Haggadah. I. Szyk, Arthur, 1894–1951.
II. Sherwin, Byron L. III. Ungar, Irvin.
BM674.643.S982 2010
296.4'5371—dc22

                              2010030980

This edition is based on the 2008 luxury limited edition of *The Szyk Haggadah*, published by
Historicana. For more information, visit www.szyk.com.

All Arthur Szyk illustrations reproduced with the cooperation of the daughter of the artist, Alexandra Szyk
Bracie, and Paul and Sheri Robbins. The digital files were edited by Stephen Stinehour and Fletcher
Manley at Stinehour-Wemyss Editions in Lunenberg, Vermont, and Rick De Coyte at Silicon Gallery
Fine Art Prints in Philadelphia, Pennsylvania, in the presence of the original artwork made available to
the project by The Robbins Family Collection. The design is based on the work of Irene Morris, Morris
Design, Asheville, North Carolina.

Printed and bound in China
10 9 8 7 6 5 4 3 2 1

Abrams books are available at special discounts when purchased in quantity for premiums and
promotions as well as fundraising or educational use. Special editions can also be created to
specification. For details, contact specialmarkets@abramsbooks.com or the address below.

ABRAMS

THE ART OF BOOKS SINCE 1949

115 West 18th Street
New York, NY 10011
www.abramsbooks.com

CONTENTS: Commentary

I. INTRODUCTION

A. What Is Passover?

Passover is the most distinctive Jewish holiday. Preparations for Passover are more intricate, complicated, lengthy, and unique than those for other festivals. Diet is radically changed to include certain foods and to exclude others. Dishes and utensils are changed. An unusual meal is served—the Seder (meaning "order")—in which fifteen choreographed steps are enacted in a specific sequence. The Seder has its own liturgy, the Haggadah.

Passover celebrates the most formative event in Jewish history, the event that birthed Israel as a people: the Exodus (see Szyk illustration on right). The prime directive of Passover is the telling, study, discussion, and transmission of a particular story—the story of the redemption of the people of Israel from Egyptian bondage. The success of Passover observance is determined by whether, through everything we say and do during the festival, this story and its meaning and message have been transmitted and "passed over" to subsequent generations. Despite all of this, or perhaps because of this, the Seder has been and continues to be the most popularly observed Jewish practice. More Jews observe Passover in some form than any other Jewish holiday; more Jews have participated in a Seder than any other Jewish ritual; more Jews have read the Haggadah than any other Jewish book. It has been estimated that more than 90 percent of American Jews have attended a Seder—more than have been *Bar* or *Bat Mitzvah*, more than observe the Sabbath or Jewish dietary laws, more than attend services for the high holydays. Passover seems to have something for everybody. Yet, as we shall see, Passover is all this, and much more.

When the Holy Temple stood in ancient Jerusalem, pilgrims would travel there to participate in sacrifices on the three harvest festivals: Passover, *Shavuot*, and *Sukkot*. Of these, the largest numbers came on Passover. Even back in days of antiquity, Jews who could not come to Jerusalem on Passover observed a Passover meal at home where they ate roasted lamb, *matzah*, and bitter herbs, and at which they recited psalms in praise of God's redemptive acts. After the destruction of the Temple, this practice evolved into the Passover Seder, in which earlier elements of the meal were retained and newer practices added. Eventually, a special liturgy called the Haggadah developed for the Seder meal.

The festival is known by a variety of names. Coming at the onset of spring and the time of the spring harvest, Passover is known as the Festival of Spring (Exodus 13:4). However, its other names relate to the primary meaning ascribed to it throughout Jewish history, all of which relate to the story of oppression and redemption, slavery and liberation, exile and exodus. The holiday was already called *Ḥag ha-Matzot*, "Festival of the *Matzot*," in the Bible (Exodus 13:3, 23:14, 34:18; Leviticus 23:6; Deuteronomy 16:16; 2 Chronicles 8:13, 30:21, 35:7); the *matzot* represent the food prepared and eaten in haste when the Israelites were liberated from Egypt suddenly (Deuteronomy 16:3). In the Passover liturgy, developed by the Talmudic rabbis, Passover is called *zeh-mahn ḥei-roo-tei-noo*—"the time of our freedom."

"Passover" is a translation of another Hebrew name for the festival: *Pesaḥ*, which has a variety of referents, including the way that God is said to have literally passed over the homes of the Israelites during the tenth plague, sparing the lives of the firstborn sons of the Israelites, unlike those of the Egyptians (Exodus 12:26–27). "*Pesaḥ*" also denotes the Paschal sacrifice offered in the Temple to commemorate the sacrificial Paschal Lamb

slaughtered in Egypt whose blood was smeared on the Israelite doorposts to avert the destruction of Israel's firstborn sons, and the subsequent Exodus (Exodus 12:1–20). Much later on, a biblical commentator stated that "*Pesaḥ*" may be interpreted as *peh* and *saḥ*, "fluent speech," thereby representing Passover as a feast of words and food where the story of the Exodus is told, studied, and transmitted. Passover became a festival focused upon the memory, the telling, and the transmission of the memory, the message, and the meaning of the story.

How the story of the Exodus was to be remembered, conveyed, and internalized became the task of subsequent generations who developed the Seder, composed the Haggadah, and celebrated the festival, from ancient times until today. How to tell the story is the continuing challenge that confronts each of us, every year, as we sit down at the Seder to celebrate the Passover festival.

B. What Is the Passover Haggadah?

The Passover Haggadah has been issued in more editions and has been read by more Jews over the centuries than any other Jewish book. Since the beginning of the printing of books with movable type in the fifteenth century, over 5,000 different editions of the Haggadah have been published. The first printed edition appeared in 1482. The most popular edition has been the *Maxwell House Haggadah*, of which some 55 million copies have been published since its first edition in 1934.

Haggadah is a Hebrew word that means "telling." It focuses upon the transmission of the story of Passover. The Haggadah is read, sung, and discussed at the Passover meal, called the Seder. The Seder takes place the first two nights of the Passover festival. In Israel, the holiday is celebrated for seven days, but Jews in the Diaspora observe the holiday for eight days. Reform Jews celebrate Passover for seven days.

Many parts of the Haggadah are unique to Passover. However, some of the prayers are appropriate for any meal, such as the Grace After Meals. Some sections, though unrelated to Passover, have become part of the Haggadah, including the song "Eḥad Mee Yoh-dei-ah," or "Who Knows One?"

The text of the Haggadah may be compared to an archaeological dig, with its many historical layers. The first layer, represented by the many biblical texts and traditions cited throughout the Haggadah, is derived from the Bible. The second historical layer reflects the times when the Paschal sacrifices and other early Passover practices were still observed at the Holy Temple, prior to its destruction by the Romans in 70 CE. After the destruction, the early Talmudic rabbis—through the interpretive process—engineered the critical and difficult transition of Passover observance from the Temple sacrifice to the home-centered celebration we know as the Seder. Yet, by the end of the Talmudic period in the sixth century, the liturgy for the Seder—developed by the early rabbis in Israel and by the later Talmudic rabbis in Babylonia—still lacked final structure and form. Beginning with the subsequent Geonic period (the seventh century to the eleventh century), the prayer book and special liturgies such as the Haggadah were standardized, taking on much of their present form and content. Subsequently, during medieval times, various hymns, songs, practices, customs, and other features were added to the Haggadah's developing text and to the way the Seder is conducted.

The Haggadah first appears in a form near to its present iteration in the writings of Rabbis Amram Gaon and Saadya Gaon by the tenth century. The process of revision, elaboration, commentary, and embellishment continues even

today, as new versions, commentaries, translations, and representations of the Haggadah continue to appear, with each generation adding its own imprint to the history of how the Passover story is told and how the Seder is celebrated.

C. Who Is Arthur Szyk?

Let us begin at the end: September 13, 1951, when Arthur Szyk died of a heart attack at 57 years of age. A retrospective view of his life and work would make it easy to believe that "Arthur Szyk" is a name of a school of artists who created a massive body of diverse artistic works over time, rather than the name of a single artist who lived a little more than half a century. Few people know or appreciate the broad scope, the artistic skill and diversity, or the immense output that characterizes the corpus of his work. Individuals are more apt to recognize some of his specific works while remaining unaware of the others. Indeed, there are many who readily recognize select Szyk works, but not his name. For example, some know Szyk's illustrations of the classical children's editions of *Andersen's Fairy Tales*, *Arabian Nights Entertainments*, or Chaucer's *Canterbury Tales* they read in their youth; or his portrayal of biblical figures in *Pathways Through the Bible* they studied in religious school; or the drawings and cartoons from his massive output of propaganda art demonizing America's enemies during World War II, which appeared in many places, including the covers of magazines like *Time* and *Collier's*; or his illustrated version of Israel's Declaration of Independence, which hangs in many Jewish homes and institutions; or his historical series, like the "Statute of Kalisz," which celebrated the granting of rights to early Polish Jewry; or other series such as "The United Nations," "George Washington and His Times," and the "Jewish Holidays"; or the Holy Ark at the Forest Hills Jewish Center in Queens, New York, or stained glass windows of The Temple–Tifereth Israel synagogue in Cleveland, Ohio—or, of course, the centerpiece of the *Szyk* oeuvre: *The Szyk Haggadah*.

Born in Lodz, Poland, Szyk was educated as an artist in Paris and Krakow. Later, he also lived in England and Canada, before migrating to the United States in 1940, where he lived out the remainder of his life. Throughout the 1940s, Szyk was an activist and often donated his artistic services in support of various social causes, including defending European Jewry, Zionism, racial equality, and many more. Szyk produced brochures, advertisements, and artistic backdrops for performances of plays by Academy Award–winning writer Ben Hecht (featuring a very young Marlon Brando) that aimed to make Americans aware of the plight of European Jewry during the Holocaust and of the Zionist cause.

Recent years have seen a renewal of interest in Szyk and his work, as evidenced by the growth of The Arthur Szyk Society, and the frequency of exhibitions of Szyk's works throughout the United States, as well as in Poland and Germany. New articles, exhibition catalogs, study guides, and books on Szyk and his works continue to be published. Highly recommended among these works is the definitive study of Szyk's life and art by the late art historian Joseph Ansell, *Arthur Szyk: Artist, Jew, Pole*. It is our hope than an encounter with Szyk's Haggadah will stimulate interest in his other works.

D. What Is *The Szyk Haggadah*?

Why is *The Szyk Haggadah* different from all other *haggadot*? The words of an early reviewer in 1940 still ring true: "Worthy to be placed among the most beautiful books the hand of man has produced. . . . It is no exaggeration to say that the volume, in respect to the range of problems set by

the artist's delicate and multicoloured designs . . . form[s] a unique triumph."

The Szyk Haggadah is a stunning and evocative visual commentary on the perennial and contemporary meaning of a text upon which interpretations have been written for centuries, and continue to be written today. Though timeless in their artistic virtuosity, Szyk's luminous illustrations of the Passover Haggadah also articulate his personal view of the world in which he lived, a world on the brink of war, Holocaust, and catastrophe. The text of the Passover Haggadah varies from edition to edition, place to place, generation to generation. Szyk's meticulous calligraphy of the Hebrew and Aramaic text, and the instructions he includes regarding how specific rituals should be performed, are typical of the liturgy and practices of the Polish Jewish community from which he emerged.

The tradition of illustrating *haggadot* dates back to the Middle Ages, long before the advent of commercial printing. *The Szyk Haggadah*, which follows in this tradition, was created between 1934 and 1936 in Lodz, Poland. It appeared in a limited edition in London in 1940, which was dedicated to King George VI of England.

The Szyk Haggadah is a visual commentary on the traditional Haggadah. Through his illustrations, Szyk articulated his lifelong preoccupation not only with history, but with what historical memory has to say about contemporary events. For Szyk, working in the 1930s, the message and meaning of motifs in his Haggadah were especially relevant for his times. Through art, Szyk both communicated and amplified a number of these key themes. Like the ancient rabbis, Szyk confronted the challenge of how to tell the story of Passover.

We do not know which particular edition of the Haggadah Szyk consulted when choosing the Hebrew text that he would set down in calligraphy in his Haggadah. What we do know is that the text of *The Szyk Haggadah* can be identified as a standard version of the traditional Ashkenazic Haggadah that was popular in Poland in the early twentieth century. For example, as discussed below, this version of the Haggadah text contains certain kabbalistic elements (see Commentary, pages 15–17, 42, 44).

Originally, *The Szyk Haggadah* was a project of the Cooperative Publishing Association of the Works of Arthur Szyk, Ltd. in L'viv (known as "Lwów" in Poland), Ukraine, which supported many of his works in the 1930s. Following earlier traditions of naming *haggadot*, especially illustrated editions, after the place in which they were either published or created (e.g., *The Sarajevo Haggadah*, *The Chicago Haggadah*), *The Szyk Haggadah* was going to be called *The Lwów Haggadah*.

Beginning with his *Livre d'Esther* (*Book of Esther*), published in 1925, Szyk issued a variety of books in very limited editions, first in France and later in England and the United States. These works, representing the highest quality of custom-made books, contained illustrations, calligraphy, or both. Such editions usually numbered in the hundreds, and were often only affordable for wealthy patrons. The original edition of *The Szyk Haggadah* is one such a book. Printed on parchment, only 250 were available for sale: 125 in England and 125 in America. A publishing company in England, the Beaconsfield Press, was organized by Szyk's L'viv supporters to publish it. To supplement Szyk's illustrations and Hebrew calligraphy, the eminent British Jewish historian Cecil Roth wrote a translation and commentary for each page of Szyk's text and drawings. The cost of each volume was about $520, which in those days was the average price for a low-end automobile—the most expensive new book of its time. This was not, however, a volume that one would use at the Seder,

exposing it to wine spills and *matzah* crumbs. In 1956 and 1957, more accessible facsimile editions were issued in Israel of about 10,000 copies each. Since then, additional printings have appeared in various formats.

In 2008, Historicana reissued a luxury limited edition of *The Szyk Haggadah*. Using new digital technology, Szyk's illustrations were restored to their original brilliance. A new, updated English translation and commentary was prepared by Byron L. Sherwin, with a creative, multicolored page layout. This edition was limited to a printing of 300.

E. Using This Haggadah

The present edition of *The Szyk Haggadah* reproduces Szyk's illustrations and calligraphy with their original clarity, crispness, and beauty. However, a new challenge had to be addressed: Can the now-classic Szyk Haggadah actually be used at the Seder? Consequently, this edition aims at making *The Szyk Haggadah* available, accessible, and usable. To achieve these goals, the translations have been somewhat abridged, focusing on the sections of the Haggadah that most people actually recite, while at the same time not eliminating any of the Hebrew that is found in Szyk's calligraphied text. Translated sections of the Haggadah are in boldface, sometimes with bracketed words to help convey the meaning of the text to the English reader. For those who cannot read Hebrew, certain sections have been made available in transliteration.

Szyk included instructions in Hebrew for conducting the Seder; however, in this edition we have built on his text in order to provide language that is clear and complete. Instructions are provided in italics, and short explanations have also been added when necessary. Also, various prayers and practices that are customarily recited and observed today have been added, such as blessings over the festival candles (see Commentary, pages 44–48). This Commentary contains much vital information that can be used in conjunction with discussion of Passover, the Seder, the Haggadah, and Szyk's visual commentary to the Haggadah.

Seven of the full-page illustrations have been moved to this Commentary section, where explanations of most of Szyk's drawings can also be found.

We have transliterated various Hebrew texts in the Haggadah and below (see Commentary, pages 44–48), for a number of reasons: (1) Szyk's Hebrew calligraphy is sometimes elusive, (2) the transliterated text is spoken aloud at the Seder, but many do not know Hebrew well enough. Rather than adapt an existing method of transliteration, we have employed our own system of transliteration which should prove accessible to the English speaker. Note that *ḥ* and *kh* are pronounced like the guttural *h* in "loch"; *ei* is pronounced like the *a* in "ale"; and we have often added the letter *h* to vowels to have a more correct pronunciation of various Hebrew words, such as *ah*, which is similar to the Jamaican pronunciation of "man" as "mahn."

As has been noted, this new edition of *The Szyk Haggadah* has been preceded by two others: the original edition in 1940, and the 2008 Historicana luxury limited edition. In response to the inevitable question of which of these three editions is *The Szyk Haggadah*, the answer is: all of them.

II. PASSOVER FOODS

A. Kosher for Passover

The laws of Passover are complex, especially those relating to food and the rules that govern what is "kosher for Passover." To make matters even more complicated, dietary practices on Passover differ among Jews, often depending upon their

family's country of origin. It is always best to consult a rabbi knowledgeable in this area of Jewish practice.

The general rule set down in the Bible is that no leaven should be eaten during the entire festival of Passover. Leaven, or *ḥameitz* in Hebrew, refers to that which ferments upon decomposition. Generally, this applies to five species of grain: wheat, barley, spelt, rye, and oats. Grains that do not ferment are not considered to be *ḥameitz*. As a fermenting agent, yeast is not used on Passover. *Matzah* is eaten because it is not allowed to ferment, or rise. Most contemporary authorities in Jewish law limit the time for preparing *matzah* to a maximum of eighteen minutes, thereby stifling fermentation.

Derivatives of the five grains are forbidden on Passover, which includes hard liquor such as scotch and whiskey and beverages such as beer. Today, items are available that are marked "Kosher for Passover," which alleviates the effort of having to decide whether an item is permitted or not. Fruits and most vegetables are usually kosher for Passover and need not be labeled. Most milk products and natural juices (without additives) are also kosher for Passover. The laws of what is kosher for Passover are an add-on to the regular Jewish dietary laws, and not a substitute for them. Foods forbidden at any time, like pork, and the prohibition of mixing meat and dairy products, remain unchanged during the Passover observance.

European or Ashkenazic Jews usually limit their use of flour on Passover to *matzah* meal (i.e., ground *matzah*) and potato flour. As a matter of custom, Ashkenazic Jews usually refrain from legumes. Rice, corn, beans, peas, peanuts, and other foods designated as *keetneet* are usually not eaten by Ashkenazic Jews, but Sephardic Jews do not observe these restrictions.

Many Jews have separate sets of pots, pans, dishes, cups, utensils, etc., that are used for Passover and have never come into contact with *ḥameitz*. Other cooking vessels, particularly those that are nonporous (and therefore have not absorbed *ḥameitz*), can be made kosher for Passover by scorching them with fire or boiling water. Some people run these items through a dishwasher (with special racks for Passover) a number of times. Glass—which is not a porous material—can be soaked and cleansed to become kosher for Passover. Ovens are scoured and left on for an extended period to rid them of any residue of *ḥameitz*.

On the night before the Seder, the search for *ḥameitz* occurs. (However, if the first Seder night is a Friday or Saturday night, *ḥameitz* is collected on Thursday night.) As in the spiritual quest itself, the focus is on the searching rather than the finding.

The next morning, the *ḥameitz* is destroyed, usually by burning. In observant homes, a legal formula in Aramaic on the nullification of *ḥameitz* is recited (see Haggadah, page 6). Consistent with Lurianic kabbalistic custom, ten pieces of *ḥameitz* are placed throughout the house, with each representing one of the ten divine powers or attributes called *sefirot* (see Commentary, pages 15, 42, 44). This process is repeated in other places where we habitually "dwell," i.e., business offices.

But what if there is too much *ḥameitz* to dispense of? What if actually surrendering or destroying all our *ḥameitz* would incur considerable financial loss? This question became especially relevant in late medieval central Europe, when one of the few trades available to Jews was the liquor business—liquor being *ḥameitz*. The rabbis addressed this problem by means of a "legal fiction." If the *ḥameitz* was not owned by a Jew during Passover, the problem would be resolved,

at least technically. Therefore, Jews "sold" their *ḥameitz* to non-Jews for the duration of Passover. Such *ḥameitz* was "sealed off," or locked up, and was in the "possession" of the non-Jew during Passover. After Passover, ownership was restored to its Jewish owner. Eventually, this "legal fiction" was extended to a stock of *ḥameitz* (e.g., liquor and foodstuffs) in one's own home. Today, it is customary to issue a "power of attorney" to one's rabbi to "sell" the *ḥameitz* of congregational members to a non-Jew for the duration of Passover. In this way, the laws are technically observed, the stock of *ḥameitz* need not be wasted, and fiscal loss is avoided.

Already in the rabbinic literature, the "evil inclination" in each of us is compared to the "leaven in the dough" (see *Genesis Rabbah* 34:10). In the Middle Ages, leaven was further allegorized to symbolize our impure thoughts and actions. In medieval sermons and ethical treatises, we find the view that the task on Passover is to remove the physical *ḥameitz* from the house and the spiritual *ḥameitz* from the self. The Rabbi of Kotzk, for example, once said that we eat horseradish on Passover to fulfill the commandment of burning the *ḥameitz* out of the body just as we burn the *ḥameitz* accumulated in the house. According to such teachings, we must take care to rid ourselves of our internal *ḥameitz* in the self through searching for it in every nook and cranny of the soul, and then by eliminating it through introspection, repentance, and good deeds.

B. The Seder Plate

The Talmudic rabbis required certain foods to be present on the dining table during the Passover meal. Some, like *matzah* and *mah-rohr* (bitter herbs), are already mentioned in the Bible; others, like *ḥaroset*, were mandated by the rabbis. Exactly which foods these were has been a matter of some confusion. Though certain foods were mandated, the rabbis did not specify how they should be placed on the table. For example, some practices place the egg and the shank bone at the top of the plate, while others place them at the bottom. Most practices include vegetables such as *karpas*, though others do not. No single configuration became the standard.

The configuration of the Seder Plate depicted by Szyk (see Haggadah, page 8) reflects the teachings of the sixteenth-century kabbalist Rabbi Isaac Luria. In his commentary to the authoritative Jewish legal code, the *Shulḥan Arukh* (see *Oraḥ Ḥayyim*, 473:4), called *B'eir Hei-teiv*, Rabbi Yehudah ben Shimon Ashkenazi, an eighteenth-century Polish rabbi, states that the configuration set forth by Luria ought to be adopted. Being a kabbalist, Luria insisted that ten items be represented in a certain configuration, with each item corresponding to one of the ten divine attributes or powers called *sefirot*. The six items on the plate, plus each of the three *matzot*, plus the plate itself, are taken to represent each of these ten *sefirot*. Let us examine what each is:

Bei-tzah is a hard boiled or roasted egg. It serves as a vestige of the *Ḥagigah*, or festival sacrifice, offered at the Temple on festivals such as Passover. It is customary to burn part of the egg's shell as a reminder of the destruction of the Temple through burning. Unlike some other items on the plate, its symbolic meaning is not discussed (as is the case for the *mah-rohr*) during the Seder. Eggs are a staple of the Passover diet. Many Jews customarily eat a hard-boiled egg at the Seder.

Z'roh-ah, the shank bone, is a symbol of the Paschal sacrifice, which was discontinued after the Temple was destroyed. It is customary to use the shank bone of a lamb. If a shank bone is not avail-

able, some use a chicken neck. In recent years, some vegetarians use a banana or a vegetable such as zucchini. In a text from the Mishnah (*Pesaḥim* 10:5) repeated in the Haggadah, the early Talmudic rabbi Rabban Gamliel required the following three foods at the Seder: *Pesaḥ*, *matzah*, and *mah-rohr.*

Pesaḥ refers to the meat of the Paschal sacrifice. Those who participated in the Paschal sacrifice at the Temple would eat of it within the Temple precincts. We know that when the Temple stood and even after its destruction, Jews would eat roasted lamb on Passover in their homes to commemorate the Paschal sacrifice. This custom is still observed among many Jews of Middle Eastern origins. However, other Jews, especially those of European ancestry, do not eat lamb on Passover in acknowledgment of the Temple's destruction and the discontinuance of the Paschal sacrifice (*Arba-ah Toorim—Oraḥ Ḥayyim*, 476*)*. The shank bone, however, remains on the plate as a reminder of what once was. Even when referring to the Paschal sacrifice during the Seder, it is customary neither to eat, hold, nor even point to the shank bone (as we do with other items such as the *matzah* and *mah-rohr*). In Rabban Gamliel's description of the "Hillel Sandwich," lamb is designated as one of its components, but today it is not eaten as part of the "Hillel Sandwich."

Mah-rohr are bitter herbs. Today, it is customary to use raw horseradish, either whole or grated. However, certain kinds of lettuce (usually romaine) were originally used on the Seder plate, since as it ripened, the lettuce leaves became bitter. As the *Jerusalem Talmud* (*Pesaḥim* 2:41) observes, like the lettuce that is initially sweet but later turns bitter, the Egyptians were at first kind, but later made the lives of the Israelites bitter through oppression and slavery.

Ḥazeret is lettuce. As has been noted, romaine lettuce was the original *mah-rohr*. But, because the *Talmud* is unclear as to whether there should be both lettuce and other bitter vegetables on the table, and since in many countries horseradish came to be used for *mah-rohr*, a custom developed to place both on the Seder plate, and to use both during the Seder. Eating a bitter herb at the Seder as a reminder of the bitterness of slavery is of biblical origin and was standardized in the *Talmud* (e.g., Exodus 12:8, Numbers 9:11, *Mishnah, Pesaḥim* 10:5).

Karpas is a leafy vegetable eaten at the Seder before the meal as an appetizer. Eating *karpas* is a rabbinic tradition, not mentioned in the Bible. *Karpas* is a reminder that spring celebrates new beginnings, and that Passover is the Festival of Spring. *Karpas* is used in the third part of the Seder where it is customarily dipped in saltwater representing the splitting of the Sea of Reeds (the Red Sea), or in vinegar representing the harshness of slavery. Following Lurianic kabbalistic tradition, it is customary to use parsley. In eastern Europe, where green vegetables such as parsley (or romaine lettuce) were not often readily available, vegetables such as potatoes, radishes, or celery were often used. The custom of using such alternatives is still practiced by some Jews of eastern European origin.

Ḥaroset, not mentioned in the Bible, is first mentioned in the *Talmud* (*Mishnah, Pesaḥim* 10:3). Rabbinic law does not consider eating *ḥaroset* to be a commandment. Therefore, unlike when eating a vegetable, bitter herbs, or *matzah*, a blessing is not recited when eating *ḥaroset*. It is customary to dip the bitter herbs into the *ḥaroset*, especially in forming the "Hillel Sandwich." There are many recipes for *ḥaroset*, most including red wine, nuts,

apples, honey, and spices such as cinnamon. The appearance of ḥaroset is supposed to resemble the mortar arduously tread by the Hebrew slaves in building for the ancient Egyptians, and the blood they shed when doing so.

C. Matzah

Matzah is the food most closely identified with Passover. Indeed, Passover is called "The Festival of the *Matzot*." *Matzah* is unleavened bread. Made from the simplest of ingredients—flour and water—it is quickly baked. *Matzah* may be the original "fast food."

Because of the haste with which the Israelites left Egypt, the bread they baked remained "unleavened" (Exodus 13:3, 6–8). *Matzah* is, therefore, a symbol of Passover and of the liberation from Egypt (*Mishnah, Pesaḥim* 10:5, based on Exodus 13:7–8).

Three *matzot* are usually placed on or near the Seder plate. Two are used for the blessings that begin the meal. The middle *matzah* is used during *Yaḥatz*, part of which becomes the *Afikomen* (see Commentary, page 32), which is eaten to formally conclude the Seder. In Lurianic kabbalah, these three *matzot* symbolize the three uppermost *sefirot*, or attributes of God. For others, they symbolize priests, Levites, and regular Israelites. There is, however, a tradition of placing only two *matzot*, which was followed by leading rabbinic authorities such as Maimonides and the Gaon of Vilna.

Like other foods eaten at the Seder, *matzah* has been given a variety of symbolic meanings. The benefit of a symbol is that it is one concrete object that can denote many abstract ideas, including some contradictory ones. For example, the *ḥaroset* that is meant to be a symbol of bitter slavery—resembling in appearance the mortar used by the Israelite slaves—is also sweet to the taste, as it is usually made with honey and wine. This sweetness symbolizes the redemption from slavery. Similarly, the egg denotes both renewal and destruction; birth and death. We burn the egg to symbolize the destruction of the Temple. In a house of mourning, the first food customarily brought to mourners is a hard-boiled egg. Another view is that the egg, which is neither a hen nor a chick, represents a state of "becoming"; a state of what is about to be, potentiality; a transition from what is to what will yet be.

Like *ḥaroset* and the egg, *matzah* also symbolizes a variety of contradictory ideas. It is the bread of affliction, the bread of the poor, the bread of slaves, and simultaneously it is the bread of redemption and the bread of liberation.

Matzah also symbolizes simplicity. It is neither bloated nor inflated. What you see is what you get. According to Hasidic teachings, one should strive to become a "*matzah*-person": simple, honest, and without pretense.

According to rabbinic tradition, not only has Passover been celebrated with the eating of *matzah* since the time of the Exodus, but before as well. Abraham and Sarah are described as eating *matzah* on Passover and serving it to their guests. The Bible tells of three mysterious men who visit them unexpectedly. These men turn out to be angels in disguise, who come to announce the birth of Isaac. According to rabbinic legend, because that day was Passover, Abraham served them a meal that included *matzah* cakes (Genesis 18:6). In one of his illustrations, Szyk depicts this legend (see Haggadah, page 16), which is also referred to in one of the hymns at the end of the Seder (see Haggadah, pages 68–69), where we read: "Abraham fed the visiting angels cakes of *matzah* on Passover." Abraham's observance of both hospitality and of Passover is meant to be a model for his descendants.

D. Wine

Unlike *matzah* and bitter herbs, Scripture nowhere requires drinking wine on Passover. However, even before the destruction of the Second Temple, it was already customary to drink wine at the Passover meal (Jubilees 49:6). After the destruction, wine was given the prominent place in the Seder it enjoys today. Identifying wine with joy (Psalm 104:15), the rabbis said, "Now [when the Temple no longer exists], joy derives from wine" (*Talmud, Pesaḥim* 109a). To satisfy a biblical obligation to rejoice on the festival, the rabbis required the drinking of wine at the Seder. Probably affirming an already extant custom, they specifically required drinking four cups of wine (*Mishnah, Pesaḥim* 10:1), the first of which is the wine of *Kiddush,* a blessing over the wine to sanctify the occasion of the festival day.

The Talmudic rabbis endeavored to identify a biblical source as the basis for the custom of drinking four cups of wine at the Seder, and various suggestions were made. However, the dominant view was to link the four cups to four terms promising redemption from Egypt which are found in Exodus (6:6–7): "[I (God)] [1] shall take you out, [2] shall deliver you, [3] shall redeem you, [4] shall take you as my people" (see *Jerusalem Talmud, Pesaḥim* 10:7). However, some of the rabbis identified a fifth term promising redemption in the following verse (Exodus 6:8): "[I (God)] shall bring you [to the Land of Israel]." Consequently, it seemed that a fifth cup was required. A dispute ensued, but a compromise was reached. Following the view of the *Mishnah* and established practice, four cups were drunk, but a fifth cup—not drunk, was placed on the table. This became known as the "Cup of Elijah," because according to tradition, at the dawn of messianic times, Elijah—the harbinger of messianic redemption (see Malachi 3:23)—will resolve all legal disputes, such as how many cups of wine one should drink at the Seder. The tradition of Elijah visiting the Seder is of medieval origin. The term "Cup of Elijah" does not appear before the fifteenth century. Some also place a chair for Elijah at the Seder table (see Szyk's Elijah Cup, right).

Some of the rabbis retained the tradition of drinking a fifth cup as an optional rather than a mandatory practice, following the view of the Talmudic sage Rabbi Tarfon. However, some of the later rabbis, like Sherira Gaon in the tenth century and Judah Loew of Prague in the sixteenth century, continued to mandate the drinking of a fifth cup. In modern times, some drink a fifth cup to call attention to currently oppressed Jewish communities who yearn for freedom and for the opportunity to immigrate to Israel. In recent decades, this included, for example, Russian Jewry, Syrian Jewry, Ethiopian Jewry, and Yemenite Jewry.

In Jewish mystical teachings, each cup of wine symbolizes one of the aspects of God—the *sefirot*—and drinking wine at the Seder with proper intention was seen as an action that helps to create unity and balance in the supernal realm (see *Zohar* III, 95b).

III. *MAGGID*: TELLING THE STORY

The central activity of Passover is the telling and the transmission of the message and the meaning of the story of Passover. The fifth part of the Seder, which is its most lengthy part, focuses upon this activity. The Haggadah employs a variety of methods to tell the story, such as narrative and prayer, question and answer, give and take, show and tell, textual study and interpretation, discussion and debate. We may supplement these with approaches of our own, like storytelling, role-playing, and acting out parts of the story in short

skits. To the questions posed in the Haggadah, we may add questions of our own: What does it feel like to be a slave? Are there things, people, ideas, institutions, habits, relationships, jobs, health problems, financial problems, political systems that enslave us now? What does it mean to be free? How does it feel to be liberated? Who are today's oppressors?

As has been noted, Passover is not only a food-fest but also a talk-fest. The subject is the story of the Exodus. The goal is to convey that story to succeeding generations represented by children, grandchildren, other family, and guests. Everyone is obliged to participate in telling the story. As the Haggadah itself reminds us, even if we are erudite scholars, we are obliged to tell the story of the Exodus. Why?

For a story to be transmitted, it must be told; it must be conveyed from one generation to the next. For a tradition, a religion, a people to continue, its stories must be passed down—passed over—to the future. Telling this story is crucial to ensuring the continuity of the Jewish people and of the Jewish faith. But, for the story to be effectively conveyed, it must be "owned," internalized and accepted as one's own personal story. It is the "wicked" son who refuses to make the story his own. That's why the story moves from the third to the first person, from what happened to "them," to what happened to "me": "This is what the Lord did for *me*, when *I* went out of Egypt" (Exodus 13:8). The story becomes each of our own personal stories.

A. What Is the Story?

After the destruction of the Temple and the Second Jewish Commonwealth (70 CE), the practice of offering the Paschal sacrifice was discontinued. The Talmudic rabbis therefore shifted the focus of Passover observance from the sacrifice to the Seder, from the Temple to the home, from participation in the Paschal sacrifice to the study and telling of the story of the Exodus, from pilgrimage to prayer. *But how should the story be told?*

The rabbis established a storyline that substantially influenced the text and the structure of the Haggadah. According to the early Talmudic rabbis: "We begin with shame and conclude with praise" (*Mishnah, Pesaḥim* 10:4). The story begins with shame and degradation and ends with praising God for our redemption. The later rabbis debated the meaning of "shame." Three views of "shame" in early Israelite history are expressed by the rabbis (*Talmud, Pesaḥim* 116a). Not wanting to exclude one in favor of another, all are included in the Haggadah.

Right after the Four Questions are asked, the first of these three narratives is offered. It is often mistakenly considered a response to the Four Questions, but it is not. Rather, it responds to the question of how we tell the story by moving from degradation to praise. For this text, "shame" is the physical and spiritual degradation of slavery: "We were slaves to Pharaoh in Egypt, but the Lord, our God, took us out of there with a mighty hand" (Deuteronomy 6:21). To illustrate this text, *Szyk* offered a drawing that represents how art and artists can become enslaved to the policies of a totalitarian regime. Here, Israelite artists are forced by their Egyptian taskmasters to paint images of the gods of Egypt (see Haggadah, page 20). As an artist, Szyk knew well that free artistic expression is squelched when others determine what an artist can create.

This text continues to tell us that had God not liberated us from Egypt, we and our families would still be slaves in Egypt. This text expresses the fundamental message of Passover: Without the Exodus, the people of Israel would never have become a distinct people. The Exodus was the

birth of the people of Israel, the seminal event in Jewish history. It is the experience that shapes all of subsequent Jewish experience. Even the other festivals find roots in the Exodus. For example, in the *Kiddush* each Sabbath, we refer to the Sabbath as a memory, as a "commemoration of the Exodus from Egypt." The pilgrim to the Temple on *Sukkot*, the Feast of Booths, offers his first fruits to God because "the Lord freed us from Egypt" (Deuteronomy 26:8–10).

Losing one's memory means losing one's mind. To remember is to remind. Bereft of memory, one becomes detached from one's own self, from one's own community, from one's past. For Judaism, faith is memory; recall of the past is a call to faith in the present. No command to believe is stated in Scripture. Rather, memory of events in the people's past is commanded. Two such unique events shape the nature of Jewish faith: the Exodus from Egypt and the revelation of the Torah at Sinai. The revelation at Sinai is celebrated on the festival of *Shavuot*, seven weeks after Passover (see Commentary, page 48). The Exodus is the focus of Passover observance. In his classic work, the *Kuzari*, the medieval poet and philosopher Judah Halevi observed that the Ten Commandments do not begin with a creedal proposition, but with a memory of an experienced event: "I am the Lord your God that [*asher*] brought you out of the Land of Egypt, out of the house of bondage" (Exodus 20:1). Modern biblical scholars point out that the Hebrew word *asher* also means "because," and that we can translate this verse as: "I am the Lord your God *because* I brought you out of the Land of Egypt." Thus, faith is rooted in the memory of events. Memory of such events makes the past present, and the future possible. The biblical injunction that drives the conduct of the Seder is the commandment to remember the Exodus, and to transmit that memory to future generations.

The goal of the Passover liturgy and of the rituals that constitute the Haggadah and the Seder is not only that the Exodus itself be remembered and transmitted, but that it be internalized as well. In this way, our ancestors become our contemporaries, and their experiences become our own. As the Haggadah puts it, "In each generation, each individual should consider himself or herself as if he or she was redeemed from Egypt, as it is written, "This is because of what God did for *me* when *I* went out of Egypt" (Exodus 13:8).

The second and third views of "shame" come right after the Four Sons (see Haggadah, pages 24–27). The second reminds us of the shame of our ancestors having been idolaters: "Originally, our ancestors worshipped idols." The text reminds us of how Abraham rejected the idolatrous beliefs of his ancestors to embrace faith in the one God. At this point in the Seder, the nature of idolatry might be discussed: What is idolatry? Does idolatry exist today? Why is it "shameful"? Why did Abraham reject idolatry? Have we? What do we believe?

This text further reminds us that God told Abraham that his descendants would be oppressed in Egypt, but that God would redeem them. The story of redemption—the story of the Exodus—is the story of how God kept his promise to redeem the descendants of Abraham.

There is a third view. We are told of how Jacob was oppressed by Laban, his father-in-law: "My ancestor was oppressed by an Aramean" (Deuteronomy 26:5). The text tells us that Laban was potentially a more severe oppressor than Pharaoh: "While Pharaoh wanted to murder the firstborn sons of Israel, Laban wanted to destroy everyone." However, they were saved. Jacob went to Egypt, from which Israel eventually emerged triumphant. In other words, the oppression in Egypt was not the first, but established a pattern that continued

after Egypt. In the text that follows, we read: "For not one [enemy] has stood against us to annihilate us, but in each generation they stand against us to annihilate us. Yet, the blessed Holy One continues to deliver us from their hands" (see Haggadah, pages 26–27). In other words, the movement from shame, oppression, and degradation to praise for redemption—the story of Passover—is also the story of Jewish experience throughout history. It is a story that begins in the times of the patriarchs and matriarchs and continues today. Only the characters change. Each generation has its Labans and Pharaohs, and each generation experiences its own redemption. But is this really so? Is this why, since the Holocaust, some Jews no longer find themselves able to affirm God's consistent redemptive powers?

Later on in the Haggadah, psalms are recited, prayers are said, and songs are sung to express thanks to God for moving us in events throughout history "from shame to praise."

After offering three versions of how the story is told, the Haggadah turns to Midrash, the rabbinic interpretation of Scripture, the rabbis' interpretive embellishments upon the biblical narrative, particularly of the verses Deuteronomy 26:5–8. For the rabbis, study of biblical texts related to the story of Exodus is the most important element of the Seder, and of Passover observance. Indeed, for the rabbis, after the destruction of the Temple, study replaced sacrifice as the most significant act of Jewish religious experience, as the most important commandment to observe.

According to a Talmudic saying (*Ethics of the Fathers* 3:3), "If [even] three people have eaten together, but have not spoken words of Torah, [then it is] as if they have eaten of sacrifices [offered] to dead idols," which is a heinous sin. Szyk illustrates this citation on the page where the Grace After Meals begins (see Haggadah, page 48). In other words, the most crucial part of celebrating Passover at the Seder is not even food or ritual, but the study of Torah.

As part of this activity of textual study, the rabbis comment on Deuteronomy 26:8 (see Haggadah, page 31): "'The Lord brought us out of Egypt with a mighty hand, an outstretched arm, great power, and with miracles and portents.' 'The Lord brought us out of Egypt'—not by the agency of an angel, a *seraph*, or a human being, but by the Blessed Holy One, by himself and in his glory. . . . 'And I shall mete out punishments upon all the gods of Egypt'—meaning: I [God], and not a[n] [human] agent. 'I the Lord'—meaning: I am he, and no other."

This rabbinic interpretation of the biblical verse contains an answer to perhaps the greatest question about how the Haggadah tells the story of Passover: *Why is Moses not mentioned in the Haggadah?* According to this text, and to others throughout the Haggadah, God alone redeemed the people of Israel—in Egypt, before Egypt, and throughout Jewish history. It is God who brings just retribution against the perennial enemies of Israel (see Commentary, pages 33–36, 40, 42).

B. Where Is Moses?

Imagine telling the story of the American Revolution without mentioning George Washington. Imagine telling the story of Passover without Moses. Yet this is exactly what the Haggadah does. In the traditional text of the Haggadah, there is only one explicit reference to Moses, which is made in a cited biblical verse from Exodus 14:31 (see Haggadah, page 34). However, in most early versions of the Haggadah, and according to Sephardic custom, this single phrase where Moses is mentioned by name is deleted. Though the biblical narrative and rabbinic tellings of the story of

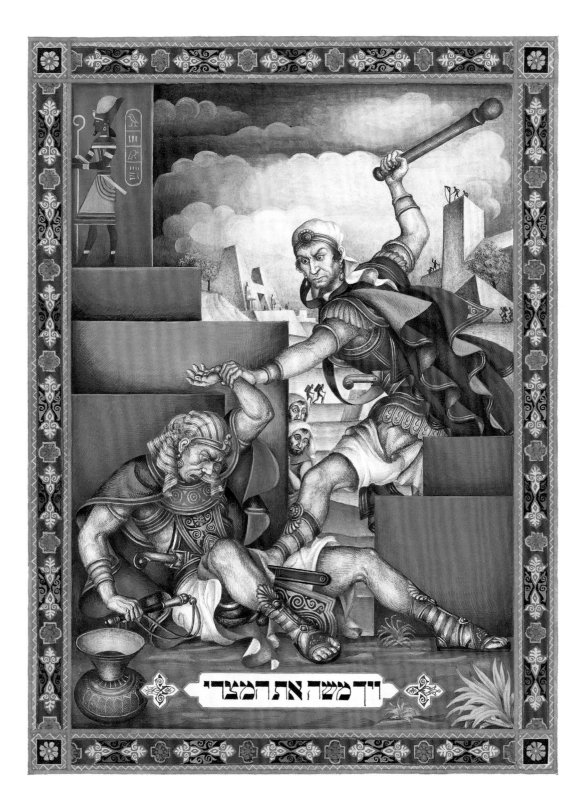

ויך משה את המצרי

Passover highlight the role of Moses as a liberator, miracle-maker, military leader, prophet, and law-giver, the rabbis who formulated the Haggadah eliminated Moses from the text.

As did previous illustrators of the Haggadah, Szyk depicts Moses' essential role in the story of Passover, but with a difference. Szyk dedicated two full-page illustrations and a number of smaller illustrations to Moses. One depicts the baby Moses (Exodus 2:1–10), drawn from the Nile by Pharaoh's daughter while his sister, Miriam, watches from the bulrushes (see Commentary, page 47). In a second full-page illustration, a muscular Moses is portrayed executing an Egyptian taskmaster for cruelly treating an Israelite slave (see previous page). Elsewhere, Szyk illustrated the first miracle Moses and Aaron perform at Pharaoh's court as part of their attempt to convince Pharaoh to liberate the Hebrew slaves—the miracle of the rod that turns into a snake (see Haggadah, page 20). Though in the Bible it is Aaron who performs this miracle, Szyk depicts Moses doing it, perhaps, once again, to emphasize the major role Moses plays in the Passover story (Exodus 7:8–12). Elsewhere, Szyk depicts Aaron, the High Priest, who wears a breastplate, signifying his office (see Haggadah, page 36). The breastplate consists of twelve sections, each representing one of the twelve tribes of Israel. Farther down on that page is the first of three panels in *The Szyk Haggadah* depicting the crossing of the Sea of Reeds, or the Red Sea (see Haggadah, page 36). Unlike other drawings that focus on the destruction of Pharaoh's army at the Sea, this one focuses on Moses' central role in the miracle of parting the waters for the Israelites, thereby allowing them to escape from Pharaoh's army, while some Israelites, still skeptical of Moses' and God's powers, look on.

Unlike the biblical text, the Haggadah recounts the "plagues of the Sea of Reeds" (see Commentary, pages 39–40) upon the Egyptians without noting Moses' agency in bringing them about. In Szyk's drawing, Moses points to the Sea, causing it to obliterate Pharaoh's legions (see Haggadah, page 36).

The section of the Haggadah that presents rabbinic interpretation of biblical texts leads into the Haggadah's discussion of the plagues brought against the Egyptians. Consistent with its view that God alone is the redeemer, the plagues are described as acts of God's just retribution upon the Egyptians. In other places in the Haggadah, God is portrayed as bringing just vengeance against all the enemies of Israel throughout history, and at the culmination of history in the messianic era (on motifs of redemption and retribution, see Commentary, pages 33–36, 40, 42). Szyk, however, literally paints a different picture.

For Szyk, human activism is required, both to bring about redemption from oppression and to bring about just retribution—even by means of violence and military action—against the enemies of Israel. Szyk portrays Moses and also David as muscular, military activists, who, through physical strength, fight the oppressor. Szyk's depiction of Moses striking and killing the Egyptian taskmaster who was brutally beating a Hebrew slave speaks to the tradition of militant, even violent, Jewish activism that he strongly advocated in his own day in combating all forms of anti-Semitism, especially the then-emerging Nazi regime.

Szyk restores Moses' place in the Passover story in his visual commentary on the Haggadah. In so doing, Szyk affirms the view of the entire Exodus narrative of the Bible, and of many of the rabbinic commentaries, which explicitly describe Moses as having a central role as God's primary agent in the liberation of Israel from Egypt. For Szyk, human activism to combat aggression, oppression, injustice is a sine qua non.

C. Study: Biblical Texts

After the destruction of the Temple, the Talmudic rabbis established study of the Torah and prayer as the most significant ways of worshipping God, now that Temple sacrifices were no longer possible. It is not surprising, therefore, that prayer and study of Torah were given an important place in the Seder. In the *Maggid* section, we encounter opportunities for study of Torah, especially of Midrash—rabbinic interpretation of biblical verses related to the Passover story—and of issues of Jewish law related to the biblical obligation to tell the story of Passover.

A section of the *Maggid* offers rabbinic interpretations on Deuteronomy 26:5–8. Deuteronomy 26:7 reads, "We cried to the Lord, the God of our ancestors, and the Lord heard our plea and saw our plight, and our misery, and our oppression." Commenting on the phrase in this verse, "and saw our plight," the rabbis said: "This refers to restraints on marital relations . . . referring to the plight of the [Israelite] male children. As it is written, 'Every male child that is born, you must throw into the river Nile, but every female may live'" (Exodus 1:22).

In other words, according to the Talmudic rabbis, besides the plight of slavery and oppression, the Pharaoh's decree of death to the Israelite male children by drowning in the Nile led couples to desist from marital relations, lest it bring about the conception and birth of a son. The plight of this disruption in marital relations was a particular form of oppression in that men were afraid to cohabit with their spouses. However, according to various rabbinic legends, the women, who were less fearful than the men, and who realized the implications of precluding the birth of a new generation, took matters into their own hands. They lured their husbands into the field, seduced them with aphrodisiacs, and became pregnant. Later on, the women would return to the fields, where they would give birth. If the baby were a girl, she would take the child home. But if the baby were a boy, she would leave the child in the fields, where they knew that God would protect and care for the child. According to one legend that *Szyk* portrays, God made milk and honey run from the rocks (see Haggadah, page 48), and the babies received their sustenance by sucking on the rocks (see *Talmud, Sotah* 11b).

D. Study: Jewish Law

One example of a legal issue raised in the Haggadah for study at the Seder relates to the biblical commandment to tell the story of the Exodus, which is the underlying commandment of the Seder itself. Though we are commanded to tell the story and to convey it, the biblical text does not specify *when* to do so. How do we know that the Seder is the appropriate time to do so? According to one view, the best time to do so could be the beginning of the month of Nissan, the month in which the Exodus took place. According to another view, it might seem that the story should only be told during daytime, but not at night—when, in fact, the Seder takes place. After all, the Paschal sacrifice was made at the Temple during daytime on the eve of the Passover. During the time of the Temple, the Seder was not yet formalized, and such issues needed resolution.

The first text in the Haggadah that relates to this issue tells of a group of rabbis who gathered to discuss the Exodus for an entire night (see Haggadah, pages 22–23). The second text, left untranslated in the Haggadah section for economy of space, is the following (see Haggadah, page 24), based upon Exodus 12:

"One might conclude that [the telling of] the narrative of the Exodus should begin with the New Moon [that is, with the first day of the

month of Nissan, rather than with Passover on the fourteenth of Nissan.] [However, such is not the case. Why?] Because Scripture says, 'You shall explain to your child *on that day*' [namely, on the day of Passover] (Exodus 13:8). Yet, one might interpret this to mean [that 'on that day' means only] in the daytime [rather than in the evening when the Seder is held]. But the biblical verse also says, 'because of *this*' [that is, 'because of what the Lord did for me when I went out of Egypt'], which refers to an occasion when the *matzah* and the bitter herbs are actually placed before you [that is, in the evening, at the Seder]."

This second text comes soon after the Four Sons, and seems out of place and somewhat irrelevant to its context. Is it?

As has been noted, when the Temple stood and was functioning, the Passover celebration focused on the Paschal sacrifice. However, when the Temple was destroyed, the rabbis faced a major challenge: Could Judaism continue without the Temple? After all, the Temple and the sacrifices given there had been the focus of Jewish religious practice for centuries. Specifically, they confronted the question of how Passover could be observed without the Paschal sacrifice.

When the Temple stood, it served as the epicenter of Jewish religious practice. The most significant religious action one could perform was offering or participating in the sacrifices. The most important religious functionary was the priest who offered the sacrifice. After the destruction of the Temple by the Romans in 70 CE, the early Talmudic rabbis redefined Jewish practice in response to the new realities. The book, i.e., the Torah, now became the epicenter of Judaism. Study of the Torah became the most significant religious action. The sage or rabbi, who interprets the Torah and tells us what it means, became the most important religious functionary.

Many read the first text, the story of the Talmudic rabbis at B'nai Brak, as a nice but superfluous story. However, this story is significant because it reflects the transition to a post-Temple Judaism. With specific regard to Passover, it represents the transition of Passover from being based on the Paschal sacrifice to its becoming a festival based on the study and telling of the Passover story. It also represents a transition of the Seder from a meal centered on the Paschal lamb to the Seder as a study and talk-fest, as well as a food-fest.

As has been noted, the rabbis responded to the question of *how* to tell the Passover story in a number of ways. The question these two texts address is that of *when* to tell the Passover story. These are questions of Jewish practice and law that are based upon interpretation of the biblical text.

According to the second text, one might conclude from the Bible (Exodus 12) that one should begin to tell the story of Passover from the first day of the month of Nissan, i.e., the month in which the Exodus took place. But based on Exodus 13:8, the rabbis conclude that the story should not be told beginning with the first day of Nissan, but with the beginning of the festival of Passover in the middle of the month, at the Seder. This establishes the legal precedent for telling the story of Passover at the Seder.

The first text deals with the question of whether the story of Passover can be mentioned at night or only during the day. A verse in Deuteronomy 16:3 says, "You should remember the day of your Exodus from Egypt all the *days* of your life." The question posed is whether the word "days" means only during the day, or also during the night. This touches upon another issue.

In the *Shema*, there are three paragraphs. The third paragraph mentions the Exodus (Numbers 15:41). At one point, the rabbis were uncertain as

to whether the third paragraph should be recited in the evening or only during the daytime. They concluded that since the word "day" also includes the night, it should be recited at the evening as well as at the morning service. This ruling established the precedent for mentioning the Exodus at night. Since the Seder is conducted at night, this precedent was applied to the Seder, thereby deeming it permissible to discuss the Exodus at night, at the Seder. Indeed, this decision made the Seder possible, and was crucial in engineering the transition of Passover from a sacrificed-based celebration to the Seder-based practice that we have today.

IV. WHAT ARE THE FOUR QUESTIONS?

In the Haggadah, several things come in fours: four cups of wine, four sons, four questions. The Four Questions are rooted in early Talmudic literature (*Mishnah*, *Pesaḥim* 10:4) and were subsequently developed into their present form, though the text and order of the questions differ somewhat insofar as Ashkenazic and Sephardic renditions are concerned. Beginning in medieval times, it became customary for the youngest child present to ask the questions. But are there really four questions, and what are they?

It has become customary to translate the first sentence of the Four Questions as a question: "Why [*Mah*] is this night different from all other nights?" However, this would give us five rather than four questions. It might be suggested that a more accurate translation would be an exclamation, not a question: "How different is this night from all other nights!" Indeed, elsewhere the Hebrew word *mah* can also be translated as "how," as in the opening prayer of the daily prayer book "How goodly are your tents, oh Jacob" (Numbers 24:5). This exclamation about Passover reinforces the fact, already noted, that Passover is different from all other Jewish holidays. Throughout the Seder, the distinct nature of Passover is explained and discussed, often through question and answer. The curiosity, especially of the children, as to how Passover differs from other holidays is addressed, while the meaning and message of Passover is conveyed. The child sees what is happening and notices that things are different on Passover—on Passover night, at the Passover meal—and he or she is stimulated to ask: What is going on? What does this all mean? Until questions are evoked, until the child inquires, the parents cannot discharge their obligation to answer the child by telling the story of Passover and by explaining its meaning (Exodus 13:14).

In some early rabbinic texts and in texts of the questions found in the Cairo Geniza, there are only three questions. Nonetheless, about no other Jewish holiday are such questions asked. The text in the Mishnah differs on many points from the text in our Haggadah today. Why is this so? Primarily because the Mishnah reflects the customs of the Land of Israel, where it was composed, while the current version in the Ashkenazic Haggadah represents many of the customs of the Diaspora. This shift in many aspects of Passover rituals and the Haggadah text from reflecting the customs of the Land of Israel to those of the Diaspora began with the later Talmudic rabbis in Babylonia (today, Iraq and part of Iran), and their successors in that region and later in Europe. Let us consider some examples relevant to the Four Questions.

In the Mishnah, the third question (not found in the Haggadah today) is: "On all other nights we eat meat roasted, steamed, or boiled, but this night only roasted." In Israel and surrounding lands, the custom—in commemoration of the Paschal sacrifice—was to eat only roasted

meat on Passover, especially lamb. This custom is still observed today by many Jews of Middle Eastern origin. In contrast, among Babylonian Jews in the Diaspora, and later among Jews of European (Ashkenazic) origin, the practice of not eating any roasted meat during Passover, especially at the Seder (unless it was garnished with gravy so that it was not completely roasted) became customary. In this view, eating roasted meat, especially lamb, at the Seder might suggest that the Temple had not been destroyed.

Another example relates to the fourth question now in *haggadot*, but not found in the Mishnah: "On all other nights, we eat either sitting upright or reclining. Why, on this night, do we all eat reclining?" The custom in the Land of Israel and throughout the ancient Mediterranean world was to eat while reclining. People, especially free people (i.e., not slaves), would recline on couches on their left side, and would eat with their right hand. In Babylonia, the custom was to eat sitting upright, and not to recline during meals. That "we all eat reclining" on Passover symbolizes eating like royalty, like free people. As the medieval rabbi Eliezer of Magence wrote: "It was only the custom of royalty in the days of the early rabbis to recline on the left and to eat on the right, so they established the rule to eat on Passover in the manner of royalty—though this is not the manner in which we usually eat in this place and time."

A final example relates to the third question in our Haggadah: "On other nights, we do not dip [vegetables] even once. Why on this night do we dip twice?" This refers to dipping the parsley in salt water toward the beginning of the Seder, and dipping the bitter herbs in the *ḥaroset* before the meal. This, again, is because of differing customs in Israel and Babylonia. In Israel, the custom was to eat many kinds of vegetables as appetizers at all meals and to dip them in some kind of sauce. In Babylonia, it was not customary to eat vegetables as appetizers, nor was it customary to dip vegetables into anything else (see *Talmud*, *Pesaḥim* 116a).

V. WHO ARE THE FOUR SONS?

Who are the "Four Sons"? What is the nature of the questions they ask? What is the meaning of the answers they are given?

According to modern commentators, the "four sons" can be four children, four daughters, four types of Jews, four types of people, four types of learners, four types of parents—each with a different attitude toward learning, each with a distinct attitude toward Judaism. Some even suggest that the four are a single person who, at different times, embraces one or more of these attitudes.

The Four Sons are first referred to in early rabbinic literature, specifically in the *Jerusalem Talmud* (*Pesaḥim* 10:37) and in a midrash on Exodus called *Mekhilta de-Rabbi Yishmael* (section "*Bo*," Chapter 18). These texts differ in some significant ways from the version that appears in our Haggadah. We shall examine how these texts shed light on a variety of features of the Four Sons of the Haggadah.

First, let us look at the identities of each of the Four Sons. According to the Haggadah, they are: wise, wicked, simple, and the one who does not know how to ask. The wise is learned, but always wants to know more. The wicked rebels and rejects tradition. The wicked may or may not be intelligent or learned, but he is not wise. In the *Mekhilta*'s version of the text, the second is not described as wicked but as obnoxious (*hahs*), which may be a better and more accurate designation of the attitude he represents.

According to the Haggadah and the *Mekhilta*, the third is "simple" (*tam*). This is a person who has superficial knowledge, but with little understanding of its meaning. He is not learned, and has no desire to be so. He is content with what he knows, and leaves learning, critical thinking, and intellectual pursuits to others. However, according to the *Jerusalem Talmud*, the third is not a simple person, but a foolish person (*tee-paish*). He is silly, foolish, and often draws the wrong conclusion from what he knows and acts accordingly. For all these texts, the fourth is "the one who does not know how to ask."

These texts articulate the pedagogic wisdom that every teacher knows: The educational process begins with the nature of the student rather than with the nature of the subject matter being taught. The teacher—the parent—must respond, not only to different types of questions, but also to different types of questioners. Yet in certain cases, such as with the fourth son, the teacher is left no choice but to initiate the learning process for the student.

The first three of the four are each described as posing a question. Based upon his question, the wicked or obnoxious son is condemned, though the wise son is not. Let's examine their questions. Unlike the third and fourth sons, the wise and wicked sons each cite a biblical verse as his respective question, indicating that both may be learned. The wise son asks: "What is the meaning of the statutes, laws, and ordinances that the Lord God has enjoined upon *you*?" (Deuteronomy 6:20). The wicked son asks, "What does this ritual mean to *you*?" (Exodus 12:26). Based on his question, the Haggadah observes that by saying "to you" rather than "to us," the wicked son demonstrates that he has excluded himself from the community, from the Passover experience, and is *kofeir b'eekar*, he "denies the principle" (on this term, see below).

What is problematic here is that not only the wicked son, but the wise son, too, cites a verse that ends with "you" rather than "us." Should not the wise son also be admonished? By saying "you" rather than "us," has not also the wise son excluded himself from the community? This conundrum, however, can be resolved by consulting the other texts. Both the *Jerusalem Talmud* and the *Mekhilta* cite the verse quoted by the wise son and end the verse not with the word *etkhem* ("you") but with the word *oh-tah-noo*—"us." In addition, the ancient Greek translation of the Torah called the Septuagint also reads "us." If the wise son quotes the verse this way, as these texts insist, then the distinction between his attitude and that of the wicked son becomes clear. In our translation, we follow these ancient readings as "us" (see Haggadah, page 25).

It would seem that the verse cited by the wise son originally ended with "us," but that when the Bible was codified "us" was replaced with "you"; or there originally were two readings—"us" and "you"—but the latter reading became standardized. Here, the Haggadah cites the current standard biblical text, rather than what might have been the original text. In any case, the reading of "us" rather than "you" clarifies the distinction made between the attitudes of the wise and wicked son.

By saying "you," and thereby excluding himself from the community, the wicked son distances himself from participation in the Exodus experience. He is called *kofeir ba-eekar*, a term that in rabbinic Hebrew usually means "denying the root," or denying a belief in God, the root and the foundation of Jewish faith. However, here it probably means that he denies the belief in the redemption from Egypt that is celebrated at the Seder, which is the primal, root event in Jewish history that shapes both the Jewish people and Jewish religious faith. Recall that he asks, "What

does this ritual mean to *you*?" and in the *Jerusalem Talmud*, his question is paraphrased as asking it in an obnoxious way: "What is this bother that you impose upon each of us each and every year?" This text further adds that if he had been in Egypt, "he would absolutely not have been worthy of redemption."

Finally, there are the answers given to the questions asked. According to the Haggadah, the wise son is told about "all the laws relating to Passover, including [the ruling that] nothing should be added to the *Pesaḥ* [the Paschal sacrifice] after the *Afikomen*." However, the *Jerusalem Talmud* which designates the third son as "foolish" rather than "simple," says that "one should teach him the laws of Passover, [including the ruling that] nothing should be added to the *Pesaḥ* after the *Afikomen*, and that he should not be part of one group [celebrating the Seder] and then join another group." These references to the *Afikomen* are confusing, but an attempt is made to clarify them in the discussion on pages 32–33 of this Commentary regarding the meaning of the word *Afikomen*.

VI. SZYK'S FOUR SONS

Since the inception of illustrated *haggadot*, the Four Sons have been the subject of a variety of artistic portrayals. For example, in the 1560 *Mantua Haggadah*, the "wise son" is modeled after Michelangelo's portrayal of the prophet Jeremiah in the Sistine Chapel. Beginning with the classic 1526 *Prague Haggadah*, the "wicked" or "rebellious" son is often portrayed as a soldier, dressed in a uniform and bearing weapons characteristic of the time and place of the illustrator. For Jews of the late medieval and early modern periods, the soldier represented war and devastation. For such Jews, the soldier was a symbol of Gentile power, cruelty, promiscuous violence, and oppres-

sion. However, in recent decades, especially in Israeli *haggadot*, the "wise son" is portrayed as a soldier, proudly and courageously defending the Jewish state.

Though replete with anachronisms, such as biblical figures dressed in medieval garb, Haggadah illustrations usually reflect the time, place, and conditions during which the illustrator lived. In this regard, Szyk's portrayals of the Four Sons are not unusual. They represent types that were familiar to him, and stand as a reflection of his own time and place. Szyk's portrayals of three of the sons represent typical types of Eastern European Jews that were undoubtedly familiar to him from his native Poland. His "wise" son is a yeshiva *bocher*—a perennial student of the Torah. The "simple" son is reminiscent of a well-known shtetl type. Largely untutored, and often a physical laborer, he knows what is expected of him, but leaves philosophical and theological speculation to others. He is a *prosteh yid*, a common, simple Jew. Szyk's fourth son, the one "who does not know how to ask," is reminiscent of another well-known shtetl type, the *batlan*—the idle loafer. A ne'er-do-well—often living off the dole, uneducated, and of coarse character—the *batlan* usually dressed like a Gentile and lived on the fringes of Jewish communal life.

What is unusual is Szyk's portrayal of the "wicked" or "rebellious" son, who is depicted differently in this illustration than the one in the body of the Haggadah (see Haggadah, page 24). There, the wicked son is a prosperous German-Jewish burgermeister who has jettisoned his Jewish identity to become completely assimilated into German culture and society. Undoubtedly, Szyk knew such individuals. Yet, it is Szyk's portrayal here (see right) of the "wicked" son in a Hitleresque manner that has evoked considerable interest. Some have suggested that it is Hit-

ler himself—the paradigmatic *rasha*, the wicked person. Indeed, originally, Szyk painted this figure wearing a swastika, which he later removed from the printed edition. However, it is unlikely that this figure is meant to depict Hitler. This figure, for example, is smoking, and not only did Hitler not smoke, but he would not permit anyone into his presence who did. Nor was Hitler likely to have worn such a cap, especially in public. Note also, that as in the other drawing of the "wicked" son, this figure wears a monocle, which Hitler did not. Rather, this figure, like the other "wicked" son (see Haggadah, page 24), seems to be a German Jew, so assimilated that he has become sympathetic to Nazism and has become Hitleresque. Since Szyk executed these drawings in the 1930s, when the Nazis were still consolidating their power—before the war and the Holocaust—he may have known such individuals. Indeed, there were some Jews in the 1930s who embraced many of the economic and military policies of the Nazi party, while expecting its anti-Semitic policies and Hitler's leadership to be temporary and short-lived. Szyk, however, saw things very differently.

VII. WHAT IS *AFIKOMEN*?

The meal of the Seder formally concludes with the eating of the *Afikomen* as dessert. The *Afikomen* is the portion of the *matzah* that is broken in the second part of the Seder, *Yaḥatz*. It is eaten after the meal, during the twelfth part, *Tzafoon* ("hidden"), because this piece of *matzah* is customarily hidden from the children during the Seder. The children are urged to find it and hold it for "ransom." They and the adults negotiate "payment" of a gift to the children so that the meal can properly conclude with the consumption of the *Afikomen*. These activities engage children in the Seder, and give them a vital role in its outcome. However,

nowhere in rabbinic literature is *Afikomen* identified with *matzah*. Though *Afikomen* is referred to as dessert in some texts, it is there identified with fruits and candies, but not with *matzah*.

Though today, *Afikomen* usually denotes a piece of *matzah*, in earlier times it had different meanings, which can cause confusion as to what the word *Afikomen* actually means.

In various early rabbinic texts, including early versions of the Four Questions, the children are told, "We don't add [i.e., it is forbidden to add] after the *Pesaḥ Afikomen*." What does this mean?

Unlike *matzah*, *mah-ror*, etc., *Afikomen* is not originally a Hebrew word. Rather, it is a Greek word that means "carousing." In the times of the ancient Greeks and Romans, after a festive meal it was customary for people to leave to celebrate, revel, and carouse. This included going to other homes to "party." The rabbis, however, felt that after sharing in the *Pesaḥ*—the Paschal sacrifice—such behavior was inappropriate, and should be forbidden. Furthermore, we know that in the times of the Temple, people ate together in small groups. At the Temple itself, they actually ate from the Paschal sacrifice, and after the destruction of the Temple, it became customary in Israel and surrounding countries, to eat lamb on Passover in commemoration of the Paschal sacrifice. The rabbinic admonition therefore originally meant that one should not carouse or eat with one group and then join other groups. This is clear from the *Jerusalem Talmud*'s response to the third son, noted on page 30 of this Commentary.

Afikomen is supposed to be the last thing eaten at the Seder. Today, as has been noted, it refers to a piece of *matzah*. However, in ancient times, the last thing eaten was the lamb. Later on, *matzah* replaced the lamb as *Afikomen*—the last thing eaten at the Seder. This is clear, for example, from the Sephardic custom of reciting

the following before eating the *matzah* as *Afikomen*: "[This is eaten] in memory of the Paschal sacrifice which was eaten when a person's appetite was satisfied."

VIII. PERENNIAL ENEMIES, ONGOING OPPRESSION

The central activity of Passover is the transmission of the story of the Exodus, which begins with oppression and ends with redemption. Throughout the Haggadah, the oppressive slavery in Egypt is discussed. However, though the Haggadah focuses upon oppression by the Egyptians, it also reminds us that "not just one [enemy] has stood against us to annihilate us . . ." Indeed, throughout Jewish history, there have been numerous examples of oppression, including pogroms, forced conversions, expulsions, various forms of severe discrimination, and genocide. In the Haggadah, we are told that as oppressive as Pharaoh was, Jacob's father-in-law, Laban, was even worse, because "whereas Pharaoh issued a decree [to murder] all [Hebrew] males, Laban aimed at destroying everyone."

Rabbinic tradition interpreted certain biblical figures, such as Laban, Amalek, and Haman (who was identified as an Amalekite), as perennial enemies and oppressors of Israel. In medieval Hebrew literature, biblical figures like Laban and Esau symbolized Rome, the Roman Empire, or one of various Christian regimes. Ishmael symbolized Muslim oppressors. Composing his Haggadah in the 1930s, Szyk viewed Hitler as the new Pharaoh, Haman, and Amalek, epitomizing the historical archenemies who oppress and who desire to destroy all of the Jews. Unfortunately, history proved Szyk's apprehensions to be correct. Many of his illustrations depict these perennial enemies as symbolized by Amalek.

Scripted with the verse "A leading nation is Amalek, but its fate is to perish forever" (Numbers 24:20), Szyk (see Haggadah, page 60) portrays an Israelite warrior girded for battle against Amalek, the archenemy of the people of Israel, and the symbol of Israel's adversaries throughout its long history. For Szyk, each generation of Jews, including his own—especially his own—must wage war against the perennial enemy of Israel.

Soon after the Exodus, Israel was attacked without provocation by its new enemy, Amalek. According to the biblical narrative, Moses stationed himself at the top of a hill, while Joshua took hand-picked soldiers to engage the enemy in Israel's first military action as a free people. As long as Moses held his hands aloft, the Israelites would prevail; when he lowered them out of weariness, the enemy (i.e., Amalek) prevailed. Aaron and Hur come to support Moses' arms for the rest of the battle. Consequently, the Amalekites are subdued. This scene (see Exodus 17:8–13) is portrayed by Szyk (see Haggadah, page 58). Inscribed on this drawing are these words: "He [Moses] said: Hand upon the throne of God. The Lord will be at war with Amalek in every generation" (Exodus 17:16). Also note that at the bottom of his drawing of the Elijah Cup (see Commentary, page 19), showing the perpetual conflict between Israel and its archenemy, Amalek, Szyk cites the verse (Deuteronomy 25:19): "You shall blot out the memory of Amalek from under the heavens: Do not forget!" This admonition, for Szyk, relates to Amaleks of the present as well as those of the past.

IX. REDEMPTION

The major theological theme of Passover is *geulah*, which means "redemption." The story that we are commanded to remember, to discuss, and to transmit, is a story of the redemption in ancient times

of the people of Israel from Egyptian bondage. Yet already in the Haggadah, and elsewhere in Jewish religious literature, the memory of the redemption from Egypt is linked to the expectation of a future, final redemption in the messianic era. As we shall see, other forms of redemption are linked to the redemption from Egypt by the Haggadah and its commentators, including Arthur Szyk. Nonetheless, according to the preeminent twentieth-century Jewish scholar and theologian Abraham J. Heschel, "one of the issues we have failed to teach in our schools is the issue of *geulah*—redemption. This is central to Judaism." What does the Haggadah tell us about redemption?

For the Haggadah, the paradigmatic redemptive event in Jewish history is the redemption of the people of Israel from Egyptian bondage and oppression. As oppression is an ongoing historical phenomenon, so is redemption. As the Haggadah text reminds us, in each generation enemies arise to oppress and to destroy the people of Israel, and in each generation, God "continues to deliver us from their hands" (see Haggadah, pages 26–27). Thus, redemption occurs not only once in Egypt, but throughout Jewish history. Throughout the Haggadah, an additional theme emerges, an idea rooted in Scripture, developed by the Talmudic rabbis, and embellished upon by the medievals: messianic redemption. In this view, though oppression may characterize experience at the current juncture of history, at some future time, history will come to its culmination with messianic redemption, a time when justice, peace, prosperity, and freedom will reign.

The expectation for a final redemption in the messianic era is based upon the memory of the redemption from Egypt. Redemption in the past becomes the precedent and the foundation for an expectation of redemption in the future. As Sa'adya Gaon, who produced the first "codified"

edition of the Haggadah (among other things), put it in his late ninth-century philosophical treatise, *Beliefs and Opinions* (8:1), the redemption from Egypt gives us reason and precedent to believe that God will redeem us in the future as God had redeemed us in the past from Egypt.

In the medieval hymns, songs, and *piyyutim* (liturgical poems) with which the Haggadah concludes, expressions of hope for the imminent arrival of messianic redemption abound. Throughout the Haggadah, messianic redemption is linked not only to freedom and an end of oppression, but also to the restoration of Jewish sovereignty over the Land of Israel and the restoration of the Temple in Jerusalem. For example, *Neertzah*, the fifteenth and last part of the Seder, largely consists of a paragraph from a liturgical poem by the eleventh-century rabbi Joseph ben Elem. It concludes with the words: "Oh, Pure One who dwells on high, raise up the fecund flock [of Israel]. With song speedily lead to Zion the choice of your flock—Redeemed!" This is followed by the exclamation: "Next year in Jerusalem!" The following hymn, "In the Middle of the Night It Came to Pass," written by Jannai, one of the earliest and most prominent Hebrew liturgical poets, recalls a series of redemptive events in Israel's biblical history, from Abraham to Esther, and concludes with a plea for the imminent dawning of the messianic age—a time in which the redemptive light of day will eclipse the long night of darkness, exile, injustice, and oppression. Szyk illustrates this hymn with a drawing of the biblical Ruth, the forebear of King David and eventually of the Messiah (see Haggadah, page 66).

The next hymn, "This Is the Paschal Offering," like its predecessor, recounts biblical events of redemption, from Abraham to Esther, and identifies them as occurring at the time of Passover. The hymn concludes with the hope for the

restoration of the Temple service on Passover in messianic times. Szyk illustrates this hymn (see Haggadah, pages 68–69) by reflecting upon its reference to King Belshazzar of Babylonia. According to Daniel 5, Belshazzar was punished for desecrating vessels looted from the Temple. Suddenly, strange words appear on the wall. Daniel informs the king that the words mean that he will soon die because of his many sins, and that his kingdom will be defeated and divided among his enemies. That night, the king is assassinated. Following this hymn is the popular fourteenth-century song "Adeer Hoo," ("Mighty is He"), which expresses the assurance that God "will build his Temple soon, speedily, speedily; in our days and soon," as a sign that messianic redemption has arrived (see Haggadah, page 70).

Hope is a theological category in Judaism, and the concept of redemption represents the articulation of that hope. But, how does redemption come to be? Who brings it about? As has been noted (see Commentary, pages 22–25), the Haggadah deliberately reads Moses out of the story of Passover in order to articulate the view that God alone brings redemption. This view pervades the text of the Haggadah. Yet, there are alternatives. The approach of the Haggadah, which sees redemption exclusively as a matter of God's grace and actions, does not seem to be the dominant view within the historical context of Jewish religious thought. Rather, most Jewish teachings, including those about the Exodus from Egypt, understand redemption as a collaborative effort between God and human beings. In other words, there is a human as well as a divine role in the achieving of redemption, a partnership between God and human beings. Indeed, according to certain rabbinic and mystical teachings, human actions not only help achieve human redemption, but that of God as well. Redemption is a collabora-

tive effort whereby both God and human beings are redeemed. As one rabbinic text puts it, "'The redemption will be Mine [God's] and yours'; as if to say, 'I [God] shall be redeemed with you'" (*Exodus Rabbah*, 15:12). In this view, since God participates in human suffering, God must also be redeemed from that suffering. God needs human beings and human action to help effect God's own redemption from an undesirable condition (see Commentary, page 44).

On one extreme, we have the view of the Haggadah that redemption is supernatural and the exclusive provenance of divine grace. On the other extreme, there is the view that human redemption comes only as a result of human action, without divine assistance. In the middle, we see the perspective that redemption is a collaborative divine-human enterprise. For classical Jewish religious teachings, human redemptive activity focuses on prayer, repentance, performance of the commandments, and the cultivation of the moral virtues. However, in the humanistic, secular view, more strident sociopolitical and even militaristic action is required. With the advent of Zionism, many Jews turned away from traditional approaches. Among them was Szyk's friend and mentor Vladimir Jabotinsky, founder of Revisionist Zionism, whom Szyk eulogized as being "the greatest leader ever given to the Jewish people." As will be noted below, Szyk himself advocated a militant activism, with or without God's help.

Szyk reflects on the theme of redemption in a number of his drawings, such as his illustrations of the Grace After Meals. The first (see Haggadah, page 50) is based upon a legend found in the Talmud (*Sanhedrin* 98a). In this tale, Rabbi Joshua ben Levi sees the prophet Elijah, who, according to tradition, will announce the coming of the Messiah. The rabbi asks Elijah, "When will the master

[the Messiah] come?" Elijah responds, "Ask him yourself." "Where does he dwell?" asks the rabbi. "At the gates of Rome, where he sits among the poor and the lepers, and bandages their sores," Elijah tells him. So, Joshua ben Levi travels to Rome where he locates the Messiah, just as Elijah had told him. "When will you come?" the rabbi asks. "Today," the Messiah responds. Some time later, Joshua ben Levi sees Elijah again, and says to him, "The Messiah lied to me. He said he would come today, yet he still has not come to redeem the world." To which Elijah responds, "He did not mean that he would come on that particular day. Rather, he was quoting the first word of a verse in the Psalms (95:7): *Today*, if you would heed his [God's] voice." In other words, whether redemption comes is ultimately in our hands. If we fulfill our divinely ordained mission to observe the commandments and to perform virtuous deeds, then the Messiah can fulfill his mission to redeem the world. Only once we make the world worthy of redemption, can redemption commence.

A second drawing is Szyk's depiction of Ezekiel's vision of the valley of dry bones as described in Ezekiel 37:1–14 (see Haggadah, page 52). This text is read in the synagogue as a prophetic reading (*Haftarah*) on Passover. The inscription in the drawing reads "Prophesy over these bones" (Ezekiel 37:4). God takes Ezekiel to a huge graveyard that is strewn with human bones, and rhetorically asks him, "Can these bones live again?" God then restores the bones to become living, breathing people.

Ezekiel lived with his fellow Israelites in exile in Babylonia after the destruction of the First Temple. The people of Israel, their land, and their Temple had been decimated—reduced to rubble, like the dry bones. But God's message said that the people could be resuscitated and restored to their land with their Temple rebuilt. Szyk read this text as a message of hope: Though currently devastated and oppressed, the people of Israel will be restored to a vibrant future, including the reestablishment of Jewish sovereignty in the Land of Israel.

For Szyk, as has been noted elsewhere, redemption is not completely a divine prerogative as the Haggadah claims, but demands active human participation. As Nazism gained power in the 1930s while he was composing his Haggadah, Szyk strongly advocated a militant program of Jewish activism to address the deteriorating situation. Szyk consistently linked current affairs to the ancient Egyptian oppression and saw Zionism, especially militant Revisionist Zionism, as a proper response to the situation. Szyk felt that Jews had to fight for their own liberation. He was not content to wait for God to send the Messiah, nor was he content to wait until the messianic era for Jewish sovereignty to be restored in the Land of Israel. For Szyk, a restored Jewish state was an urgent desideratum, a modern and perhaps secular expression of an old religious idea. A State of Israel would be, for Szyk, a contemporary expression of a form of messianic redemption.

X. ISRAEL

Throughout the Haggadah, the hope for the restoration of Jewish sovereignty in the Land of Israel is expressed. According to many individual texts in the Haggadah, the process of redemption that commences with the Exodus culminates with the settlement of the people of Israel in the Land of Israel that fulfills the promise God made to the patriarchs of Israel. After the defeat of the Second Jewish Commonwealth and the destruction of the Temple by the Romans, the rebuilding of the Temple and the restoration of the Jewish state was projected onto an indefinite messianic future.

By Szyk's time, the Zionist movement was

fervently urging Jewish settlement in the Land of Israel and the reestablishment of a Jewish state. Szyk was an avid Zionist who was clearly aligned with the militant Revisionist Zionists led by his friend Vladimir Jabotinsky and later by Menachem Begin. During World War II, Szyk worked closely with the Revisionists in the United States to help save European Jews. In this effort, he collaborated with such diverse figures as Revisionist/Irgunist leader Peter Kook Bergson, the playwright Ben Hecht, and the young Marlon Brando. Szyk's illustration of Israel's Declaration of Independence hangs in many Jewish homes and Jewish institutions. In his Haggadah, Szyk's illustrations articulate his view that militaristic, activistic Jewish initiatives are required to fight oppression of Jews, and eventually to bring about the rebirth of the Jewish state. For example, toward the end of the Haggadah, to the song "Eḥad Mee Yoh-dei-ah," Szyk adds a verse from Psalms (35:3): "Ready the spear and the javelin against my pursuers, and tell me: I am your deliverance." His illustration there shows King David in his royal chariot, going into battle against his enemies. In this work, the foes of the people of Israel are symbolized by the trodden enemy soldier, and perhaps also by the eagle, a symbol of evil empires, including Rome and Nazi Germany (see Haggadah, page 74). The dove represents providential care over David and his people. The banner of blue and white undoubtedly symbolizes the Zionist movement, which was trying to establish a Jewish state at the time Szyk's Haggadah was composed in the 1930s. David's chariot of triumphant hope may be juxtaposed against Szyk's portrayals of the decimated chariots of Pharaoh's army at the Sea of Reeds (the Red Sea).

Szyk's dedication to the Zionist program of establishing a Jewish state pervades his Haggadah and is highlighted in the King George dedication page (see Haggadah, frontispiece). On the medallion drawing that begins his Haggadah, as well as on his French dedication page (see the front of this Commentary), he cites the verse from Psalms (137:5): "If I forget you, O Jerusalem, let my right hand wither."

In the English dedication page, Szyk addresses King George VI of England: "At the feet of your most gracious majesty, I humbly lay these works of my hands, shewing forth the afflictions of my people, Israel." Here, Szyk implores the king not only to combat the Nazis who oppress his people, but also beseeches him to allow the emigration of imperiled European Jewry to the Land of Israel, then under British jurisdiction and blocked by the British government. Szyk portrays himself at the corner of this drawing, dressed in a paramilitary uniform, brush in hand, going to war against the enemies of his people as "a soldier in art." He reflects his situation, as a newcomer to England with his Polish homeland already overrun by Germany, by signing his name "Arthur Szyk, Illuminator of Poland." However, on the French dedication page, he identifies himself as *Imagier* of Israel" and "a Jew praying in art."

In addition, the French dedication page shows Judith holding the head of Holofernes, an enemy of the Jewish people whom she had assassinated. This is reminiscent of Szyk's portrayal of David holding the severed head of another enemy of Israel, Goliath, in his illustration of "Ḥad Gadya" (see Commentary, page 43). In Szyk's view, the conditions of his times demanded a militant rather than a passive response to oppression. As Cecil Roth wrote in his introduction to the 1940 Szyk Haggadah, "recent events have indicated that in these days of organized brutality, nonresistance may sometimes be equivalent to suicide. . . . The traditional equation of militarism and iniquity needs correction."

XI. INDIVIDUAL REDEMPTION

During the third and fourth centuries, the *Jerusalem Talmud* reflected on the meaning of Passover. The Land of Israel, where the *Jerusalem Talmud* was composed, was then under the harsh occupation of Rome. The redemption from Egypt seemed an event of the distant past, a vague historical and theological memory, with little pertinence to the current situation. Messianic redemption was projected onto a distant future. But some relevant teaching was still sought. It was therefore taught that even in such historically hopeless times, one type of redemption still remained available: that of the individual.

Though a collective or national redemption was then politically, socially, and economically out of reach, nonetheless some kind of individual redemption was available through the performance of the commandments and the cultivation of the moral virtues. In this view, redemption was no longer restricted to national or collective destiny, because an individual could still achieve a modicum of redemption by ascending from a state of individual spiritual bondage to a state of individual spiritual redemption. This approach became prominent centuries later in Hasidic reflections on Passover, particularly during the eighteenth and nineteenth centuries. For example, according to the early Hasidic master Rabbi Menahem Nahum of Chernobyl, Passover commemorates two levels of redemption: *geulah kelalit*, that of the people of Israel; and *geulah peratit*, that of the individual person. For this rabbi, the collective redemption of the Exodus could only occur after each person had attained the spiritual state of individual redemption. In this view, not only can redemption occur in a group, but also within each individual human soul.

According to this teaching, "Egypt" and "Israel" are not only political states or geographical places, but also symbols of spiritual states of being. The spiritual state of "Egypt" is a state of bondage, enslavement, an undesirable situation from which we seek liberation; "Israel," "Zion," and "Jerusalem," on the other hand, denote spiritual states that we can attain, to which we wish to aspire. For example, people find themselves in a state of "Egypt," whether it be bondage to a bad habit, a bad relationship, or an oppressive job. On Passover, a person can begin the process of liberation from that which oppresses or that which stifles individual spiritual development. "Egypt" represents spiritual dysfunction, and redemption from "Egypt" represents liberation from that state of being. The state of "Zion," "The Holy Land," "Jerusalem," denotes spiritual fulfillment. Passover, in this view, is something that must occur on the individual level as well as the collective. It represents a transition from individual bondage to individual redemption. From this perspective, the famous declaration toward the end of the Haggadah—"Next year in Jerusalem!"—has two meanings. One relates to the redemption of the people of Israel in the future messianic age, but the other relates to the redemption of the individual in the present from the restraints that inhibit spiritual development. "Jerusalem" represents a high state of individual spiritual development, along with the hope for a future collective messianic redemption that parallels the historical redemption from Egypt.

These motifs have their roots in the *Jerusalem Talmud*. They arose at a time when the people were enduring physical, political, national, and economic oppression by the Romans in the Land of Israel. Any form of collective or national redemption seemed a distant memory and a hope projected onto the messianic future. Therefore,

two ideas were articulated: the redemption from Egypt provided assurance for the expectation of an eventual future redemption; and if a collective redemption could not be currently achieved, given contemporary conditions, an individual could nonetheless achieve some individual redemption through observance of the commandments, prayer, cultivation of the moral virtues, repentance, and engaging in a program of individual spiritual development.

XII. HOW MANY PLAGUES?

The Haggadah, based upon the biblical narrative in Exodus 3–12, describes the Ten Plagues that God brought upon the Egyptians in Egypt. The plagues are also listed in a somewhat different way in Psalms (78:44–51, 105:24–36). In their interpretations of the Exodus, the Talmudic rabbis claimed that not only did God bring ten plagues upon the Egyptians in Egypt, but that each of these plagues actually represented a "cluster" of plagues. As the Haggadah itself records this rabbinic view, each plague was actually a cluster of either four or five plagues. Hence, we discover that there were forty or fifty plagues brought against the Egyptians in Egypt. Furthermore, the rabbis claimed that God brought additional plagues against the Egyptians at the Sea of Reeds (the Red Sea). In the Haggadah itself, various rabbis debate how many such plagues there were (see also *Midrash on Psalms* 78:15, *Exodus Rabbah* 23:9). Thus, according to the Haggadah, the number of plagues at the Sea of Reeds far exceeded those in Egypt, as did the number of victims of those plagues (see Haggadah, page 34). Indeed, the Book of Jubilees (48:14) places the number of dead Egyptians at the Sea at over one million.

As has been noted, there is a custom of spilling out a little wine while reciting each of the names of the Ten Plagues God visited upon Egypt. However, there are also customs of spilling out thirteen or sixteen drops of wine. *Why?*

Rabbi Yehudah made a Hebrew mnemonic of three "words" from the first letters of the names for each of the Ten Plagues (see Haggadah, pages 33–34): *D'Tz-aKH Ah-DaSH B'A-ḤaB* (see *Sifre on Deuteronomy*, "*Piska,*" 301). There is a tradition that this mnemonic was inscribed on Moses' staff (see *Exodus Rabbah* 8:3). The custom of spilling out thirteen drops of wine comes from adding the three "words" of the mnemonic to the Ten Plagues. However, before mentioning the Ten Plagues in the Haggadah, the text tells us of three additional plagues noted by the prophet Joel (3:3): blood, fire, and pillars of smoke (which Szyk illustrates; see Haggadah, page 30). Adding the ten plagues of Egypt to the three words of the mnemonic to the three plagues of Joel yields sixteen. Also, there is an old tradition that relates the sixteen drops of wine to a midrashic tradition that God destroyed the Egyptians with a sword of sixteen blades.

Why do we spill out drops of wine at this point in the Seder? Originally, probably in the Middle Ages, it was the offering of a bribe to the "evil spirits." It was believed that evil spirits dwelled everywhere, and that they could be provoked to cause us harm. We must be on our guard from their malevolent influence. Seeing us enjoy a lavish meal, they could easy become jealous. Consequently, we are taught to "bribe" them, so they neither harm nor disturb us. In modern times, however, when people no longer believe in demons, alternative explanations have been given. Though we might no longer believe in demons per se, it would be naïve for us to believe that there are not evil and malevolent forces and persons such as viruses and terrorists all around us trying to harm us.

A popular and more recent explanation is

based upon a Talmudic text in which the angels begin singing praises to God after the decimation of the Egyptians at the Sea of Reeds. God silences the angels, saying: "The works of my hands are drowning in the Sea, and you sing hymns of praise!" (*Talmud, Sanhedrin* 39b). In other words, God reminds the angels that the Egyptians are also God's creation, the children of God. Though their punishment is deserved, it is an occasion neither for gloating nor for celebration. Rather, empathy for one's defeated enemy is what the moment requires. Spilling out wine, symbolizing tears, represents our empathy and God's distress at the Egyptian losses. It is telling that Szyk does not refer to the tradition of spilling out drops of wine when reciting the names of the plagues. For Szyk, justice and retribution without empathy is precisely what the Egyptians, and all enemies and oppressors of the people of Israel, deserve. This observation leads us directly to an examination of the theme of just retribution in the Haggadah and in Szyk's illustrations.

XIII. JUST RETRIBUTION

According to the Haggadah, just retribution against oppressors is an integral part of the process of redemption. God, who redeems the people of Israel from their oppressors, visits harsh judgments upon the enemies of Israel in reprisal for their acts of injustice and cruelty. Already in the Bible, the plagues that God brings against the Egyptians in Egypt, and later at the Sea of Reeds, exemplify such just retribution. Included in the Haggadah is the record of a debate among the Talmudic rabbis as to how many plagues God brought upon the Egyptians after the Exodus at the Sea of Reeds. According to no less a figure than Rabbi Akiva, there were not 10, 50 or 200 as his colleagues suggested, but 250 plagues at the Sea

of Reeds (the Red Sea), indicating a high level of divine retribution against the Egyptians (see Haggadah, page 34; see also Szyk's depiction of the fate of the Egyptians at the Sea of Reeds, right).

During the Elijah Cup ceremony of the Seder, biblical verses are offered as prayers, beseeching God to pour out his wrath and fury in the destruction of Israel's enemies as punishment for their malicious deeds. Szyk embellishes this text with a depiction of the devastation of the Egyptians at the Sea of Reeds (see Haggadah, pages 54–55). The custom of reciting these verses at the Seder seems to have been introduced by the Jews of France or Germany before the twelfth century in response to the harsh persecutions at that time, especially during the Crusades. One can only wonder how Szyk might have illustrated this particular page (see Haggadah, page 54) had the Holocaust taken place before he composed his Haggadah drawings.

The recitation of these verses links the memory of divine retribution against the Egyptians to the hope that God will continue to punish all those who have unjustly oppressed the people of Israel throughout their history. This theme is reiterated in the hymns and songs at the end of the Seder such as "This Is the Paschal Offering" and "Ḥad Gadya." According to various commentators, the message of "Ḥad Gadya" is that there is justice and retribution for wrongdoing; God is the ultimate guarantor of justice in the world. Such a message is reminiscent of this statement from the *Ethics of the Fathers* (2:6): "Once he saw a skull floating on the water. He said to it, 'Because you drowned others, people have drowned you, and the fate of those who drowned you is that they, too, will one day be drowned by still others.'" Or, as the rabbinic proverb puts it, "There is justice and there is a Judge." In this view, "Ḥad Gadya"—the one kid—represents the people of Israel, and the other "characters" in the song represent oppres-

sors encountered by the people of Israel throughout their history. Each, in turn, is destroyed, and God's justice triumphs at the end.

In his illustration of the Haggadah's statement (see Haggadah, pages 26–27)—that "not just one [enemy] has stood against us to annihilate us, but in each and every generation they stand against us to annihilate us. Yet, the Blessed Holy One continues to deliver us from their hands"—Szyk shows a person reciting this statement, overlooking a battlefield strewn with the defeated enemies of the Jewish people, especially Rome. Barely perceptible on the fallen crown near the wheel is the name of Israel's enemy: Haman. Above all stands the Ten Commandments, signifying the ultimate supremacy of God's law, as well as divine justice and retribution.

Throughout his Haggadah, Szyk affirms his view that retribution devoid of empathy is a deserved and just reward for the enemies of the people of Israel. For Szyk, though divine retribution is necessary, it is not sufficient. Szyk called for militant Jewish activism to combat oppressors. For example, though it is not part of the Haggadah text, Szyk depicts the biblical scene of Moses striking down an Egyptian task master for cruelly treating a Hebrew slave (see Commentary, page 23). As elsewhere in his drawings, Szyk depicts Moses here as a militant, "muscular Jew" fighting the enemies of Israel. For Szyk, human beings in general, and Jews in particular, must assume an activist approach—even a militant and violent one—to combat oppression.

Szyk's Haggadah illustrations articulate his conviction that without proactive human agency on behalf of justice and against oppression, redemption—with or without divine intervention—is not likely to occur. It is not coincidental, therefore, that Szyk illustrates "Ḥad Gadya" with the second of two depictions of David's slaying of Goliath (see right). The citation on the first reads: "David took the [severed] head of the Philistine [Goliath]" (1 Samuel 17:54). There, the Philistine is portrayed as having dark eyes, hair, and complexion (see Haggadah, page 34). Yet in the second, he has blond hair and blue eyes, undoubtedly symbolizing the enemy of the Jews during Szyk's time: the Aryan, the German Nazi. The message here, as in "Ḥad Gadya," is that justice and retribution will ultimately prevail. For Szyk, Jewish militancy and activism—of which he sees David and Moses as paradigmatic models—are the primary vehicles for meting out justice to the foes of the Jewish people.

XIV. *KAVVANOT*: KABBALISTIC MOTIFS

As has been mentioned, Szyk's configuration of the Seder plate is influenced by Lurianic kabbalah—a sixteenth-century school of Jewish mysticism based on the teachings of Rabbi Isaac Luria. Throughout his Haggadah, there is another blatantly kabbalistic element, also Lurianic in origin: *kavvanot*. A *kavvanah* is a short mystical meditation recited before saying a prayer about performing a specific sacred action, a *mitzvah*. *Kavvanot* are found throughout *The Szyk Haggadah*, though only the first—found at the bottom of his illustration of the Order of the Seder—has been translated (see Haggadah, page 11). This *kavvanah* is recited before drinking the first of the four cups of wine at the Seder. It reads: *"Behold, I am ready and prepared to fulfill the commandment of* drinking the first of the four cups of wine, *for the sake of unifying the Blessed Holy One with his Shekhinah [The Divine Presence], which is hidden and mysterious, in the name of all Israel."* The formulaic part is given here in italics. The commandment being performed is named in the remaining text: "drink-

ing the four cups of wine," "telling the story of the Exodus," (see Haggadah, page 14), "eating the bitter herbs" (see Haggadah, page 44), and "eating the *Afikomen*" (see Haggadah, page 46).

The practice of *kavvanot* relates to the kabbalistic idea of the *zee-voo-ga kah-deesha*, "The Holy Intercourse" between the "male" attribute of God, called *Tiferet* and designated here as "The Blessed Holy One," and the "female" attribute of God, called *Shekhinah*. On the Seder plate, the former is represented by the *mah-rohr* and the latter by the plate itself. In Jewish mysticism, especially in its major work, the *Zohar*, the goal of observance of the Jewish holydays is to bring about the *zee-voo-ga kah-deesha*, thereby restoring unity, balance and harmony between the male and female aspects of the Divine. In this way, the human being helps bring about redemption to God. From this perspective, known as theosophical theurgic kabbalah, human actions can help bring about the redemption of God. Here, the Passover motif is turned on its head: Instead of God redeeming us, our actions can help redeem God. This can be done by performing the most simple of sacred deeds with the right intention, such as the drinking of the four cups of wine during the Seder (see *Zohar*, III, page 95b). *Kavvanah* literally means "intention"; its purpose is to create the right intention for performing a sacred action that aims at bringing about unity and harmony within God.

Szyk hints at another example of the "Holy Intercourse" in his instructions for preparing to recite the Grace After Meals. He refers in his "instructions" to the custom of the *mayyim aharoneem*, the "latter waters," that is, using a fingerbowl of water after eating to parallel the washing of the hands with the blessing before beginning the meal (see Haggadah, page 46, bottom). In Jewish mystical teachings, the "former waters," the water used in washing before the meal are the "male" waters, and those after the meal are the "female waters," which, when brought together at the meal, bring about the "Holy Intercourse" and help restore balance and unity within the divine realm known as the *sefirot*.

XV. ADDITIONS TO *THE SZYK HAGGADAH*

A. Lighting the Festival Candles

At least twenty minutes before sunset, and before sitting down for the Seder, candles are lit, usually by the hostess, her daughters, and often also by female guests. If no females are present, males may light the candles. On the Sabbath, the words in parentheses are also recited. On the Sabbath, it is customary to cover one's eyes after lighting the candles. These two blessings are recited after the candles are lit.

בָּרוּךְ אַתָּה יהוה אֱלֹהֵינוּ מֶלֶךְ הָעוֹלָם
אֲשֶׁר קִדְּשָׁנוּ בְּמִצְוֹתָיו וְצִוָּנוּ
לְהַדְלִיק נֵר שֶׁל (שַׁבָּת וְשֶׁל) יוֹם טוֹב:

Barukh atah Adonai, Eloheinoo melekh ha-oh-lahm, ah-sher kee-d'shah-noo b'meetz-voh-tav, v'tzee-vah-noo, l'hahd-leek neir, shel (shabat v'shel) yom tov.

Blessed are you, Lord our God, Sovereign of the Universe, who has sanctified us by his commandments, and has commanded us to kindle the (Sabbath and) festival candles.

בָּרוּךְ אַתָּה יהוה אֱלֹהֵינוּ מֶלֶךְ הָעוֹלָם
שֶׁהֶחֱיָנוּ וְקִיְּמָנוּ וְהִגִּיעָנוּ לַזְּמַן הַזֶּה:

Barukh atah Adonai, Eloheinoo melekh ha-oh-lahm, sheh-heh-hee-yah-noo, v'kee-yem-ah-noo, v'hee-gee-yah-noo, lah-z'mahn ha-zeh.

Blessed are you, Lord our God, Sovereign of the Universe, who has kept us in life, who has sustained us, and who has enabled us to reach this time.

B. Blessing the Children

Children are never considered too old to be blessed by their parents. The blessing of children takes place just before *Kiddush* (see Haggadah, pages 12–13). Customarily, a parent places hands on the child's bowed head and the parent says:

For sons:

יְשִׂמְךָ אֱלֹהִים כְּאֶפְרַיִם וְכִמְנַשֶּׁה.

Y'seem-khah Elohim k'efrah-yeem v'kheem-na-sheh.
May God bless you, as God blessed Ephraim, and Manasseh (Genesis 49:20).

For daughters:

יְשִׂמֵךְ אֱלֹהִים כְּשָׂרָה רִבְקָה רָחֵל וְלֵאָה.

Y'seem-ei-kh Elohim k'sah-rah, reev-kah, raḥeil, v'lei-ah.
May God bless you, as God blessed the matriarchs of the people of Israel: Sarah, Rebecca, Rachel, and Leah (Ruth 4:11).

Some then add the "priestly blessing" (Numbers 6:24–26):

יְבָרֶכְךָ יְיָ וְיִשְׁמְרֶךָ.
יָאֵר יְיָ פָּנָיו אֵלֶיךָ וִיחֻנֶּךָּ.
יִשָּׂא יְיָ פָּנָיו אֵלֶיךָ וְיָשֵׂם לְךָ שָׁלוֹם.

Yeh-vah-rekh-kheh-khah Adonai v'yeesh-m'reh-khah.
Yah-eir Adonai pah-nahv ei-leh-khah v'y'khoo-neh-kah.
Yee-sah Adonai pah-nahv ei-leh-khah, v'yah-seim l'khah shalom.

May God bless and protect you.
May God's presence shine upon you, and be gracious unto you.
May God's presence be upon you, and grant you the wholeness of peace.

C. The Miriam Cup

In recent decades, various new rituals have been added to the Seder. One of these, introduced by Jewish feminists, is the inclusion of Miriam's Cup, to celebrate the role of women in general, and of the prophetess Miriam in particular, in the story of the redemption from Egypt. As it happens, however, in the tenth century Rabbi Sherira Gaon noted a custom of placing a third cooked dish (besides the shank bone and the egg) on the Seder plate in memory of Miriam and her role in the Exodus (see Micah 6:4).

Following the drinking of the second cup of wine (see Haggadah, page 45), a cup of water is poured into the Miriam Cup. Springwater is recommended. This relates to an ancient rabbinic legend that tells of a miraculous well of springwater that accompanied the Israelites throughout their journey in the wilderness after the Exodus providing them with fresh water (see *Leviticus Rabbah* 22:4, *Numbers Rabbah* 1:2, 13:20). This well was given to Miriam by God in honor of her bravery and devotion. A source of sustenance and healing, this well served as a portable oasis in the desert.

When the cup is filled, some say:

> **This is the well of Miriam**
> **the cup of living waters.**
> **Rise up, O well! Sing to her!**

Some also tell a story about a Jewish woman they admire after filling the cup. Some discuss Miriam's role in the Bible and in legend, and compare her role, her legend, and her cup to that of Elijah.

Others say:

> **Miriam the prophet, with the timbrel**
>   **in her hand.**
> **Miriam led us in a song of praise by the**
>   **seashore.**
> **Miriam danced with us to increase the**
>   **people's joy.**
> **Let us be worthy of salvation, speedily**
>   **and by her merit.**
> **Living waters from her well.**
> **Living waters from her well.**

Some dance and sing as did Miriam and the women at the Sea of Reeds (the Red Sea) (Exodus 15:20–21): "Then Miriam the prophetess, Aaron's sister, took a timbrel in her hands, and all the women went after her in dance and with the timbrels. And Miriam chanted for them: 'Sing to the Lord for he has triumphed gloriously; horse and rider he has hurled into the sea.'"

Recall that it is Miriam who watches out for her baby brother Moses after he is cast into the Nile. It is Miriam who makes sure that Moses is saved from Pharaoh's decree of death upon newborn Hebrew males. It is Miriam who watches until she is assured that Moses is safely in the hands of the daughter of Pharaoh. It is Miriam who convinces the daughter of Pharaoh to get Moses a wet-nurse—who happens to be his own mother, Yoheved. Hence, without Miriam, Moses would not have been saved, and the Exodus would not have occurred. Szyk depicts this scene in his illustration of baby Moses (see right), based on Exodus 2:1–10. This piece is reminiscent of the depiction of the baby Moses in the thirteenth-century Barcelona Haggadah.

Yet there is also a great irony in assigning Miriam a place in the Haggadah and the Seder. As was discussed, the rabbinic creators of the Hagga-dah eliminated Moses from how the story of the first Passover and the Exodus are told by the Haggadah. If Moses was excluded, why should Miriam be included? But if Moses is reclaimed by commentators to the Haggadah, such as in the visual commentary of Arthur Szyk, why not also include the prophetess Miriam?

D. The Psalm of Ascent: Psalm 126

This psalm is customarily recited or sung as a preface to the Grace After Meals (see Haggadah, pages 48–49).

שִׁיר הַמַּעֲלוֹת בְּשׁוּב יהוה אֶת שִׁיבַת
צִיּוֹן הָיִינוּ כְּחֹלְמִים:
אָז יִמָּלֵא שְׂחוֹק פִּינוּ וּלְשׁוֹנֵנוּ רִנָּה אָז יֹאמְרוּ
בַגּוֹיִם הִגְדִּיל יהוה לַעֲשׂוֹת עִם אֵלֶּה: הִגְדִּיל
יהוה לַעֲשׂוֹת עִמָּנוּ הָיִינוּ שְׂמֵחִים: שׁוּבָה יהוה
אֶת שְׁבִיתֵנוּ כַּאֲפִיקִים בַּנֶּגֶב: הַזֹּרְעִים בְּדִמְעָה
בְּרִנָּה יִקְצֹרוּ: הָלוֹךְ יֵלֵךְ וּבָכֹה נֹשֵׂא מֶשֶׁךְ הַזָּרַע
בֹּא יָבֹא בְרִנָּה נֹשֵׂא אֲלֻמֹּתָיו:

> **When the Lord restores the fortunes of**
>   **Zion, we shall see it as in a dream.**
> **Our mouths shall be filled with laughter,**
>   **our tongues, with songs of joy.**
> **Then they will say among the nations,**
>   **"The Lord has done great things for**
>   **them!"**
> **The Lord will do great things for us, and**
>   **we shall rejoice.**
> **Restore our fortunes, O Lord, like water-**
>   **courses in the desert.**
> **They who sow in tears, shall reap songs**
>   **of joy.**
> **Though he goes along weeping, carrying**
>   **the seed bag,**
> **he will return with songs of joy, carrying**
>   **his sheaves.**

מרחמים משׁיתהו

E. Counting the *Omeir*

In addition to celebrating the Exodus from Egypt, Passover also marks the beginning of the barley harvest. Beginning on the second night of Passover, an *omeir*, a sheaf of barley, was brought as an offering (see Leviticus 23:10–14). Since the *omeir* was reaped and prepared at night, the blessing of the *omeir* is recited at night. This counting of the *omeir* is continued for forty-nine days. The countdown begins with the second night of Passover and culminates with the festival of *Shavuot*. The counting of the *omeir* thereby establishes the link between Passover and *Shavuot*.

Shavuot is the festival that commemorates the revelation of the Torah at Mount Sinai. The counting of the *omeir* articulates the link between the redemption from Egypt and the revelation at Sinai. For the rabbis, the Exodus establishes the Jews as a people, while the revelation of the Torah provides the meaning, purpose, and raison d'être for the existence of the people of Israel. In this view, the purpose and culmination of the Exodus is vested in the giving and acceptance of the Torah. From this perspective, the ultimate purpose of the Exodus is not the return of the Israelites to the "promised land," but to provide the conditions whereby the people of Israel could fulfill their nature and mission through the obser-vance of God's laws and commandments given in the Torah at Sinai. As a rabbinic text puts it, "To deny the commandments is to deny the Exodus" (*Sifra*, "*Shemini*" on Leviticus 10:12; see also Psalm 105:44–45). According to a medieval work, *Sefer ha-Heenookh*, the people of Israel were liberated from Egypt for one primary reason: to receive the Torah at Sinai.

The following is recited toward the end of the Seder, and there are a variety of traditions as to exactly when that is; we recommend after "Adeer Hoo" (see Haggadah, pages 70–71).

בָּרוּךְ אַתָּה יְיָ אֱלֹהֵינוּ מֶלֶךְ הָעוֹלָם אֲשֶׁר קִדְּשָׁנוּ בְּמִצְוֹתָיו וְצִוָּנוּ עַל סְפִירַת הָעֹמֶר:

Barukh atah Adonai, Eloheinoo melekh ha-oh-lahm, ah-sher kee-d'shah-noo b'meetz-voh-tav, v'tzee-vah-noo, al s'fee-raht ha-oh-meir.
Blessed are you, Lord our God, Sovereign of the Universe, who has sanctified us with your commandments and has commanded us to count the *omeir*.

הַיּוֹם יוֹם אֶחָד לָעֹמֶר:

Ha-yohm yohm eḥad lah-oh-meir.
This is the first day of the *omeir*.

XVI. SELECTED READINGS

Joseph P. Ansell. *Arthur Szyk: Artist, Jew, Pole.* Oxford: The Littman Library of Jewish Civilization, 2004.

Baruch M. Bokser. *The Origins of the Seder.* Los Angeles: University of California Press, 1984.

Daniel Goldsmith. *Haggadah shel Pesaḥ* [Hebrew]. Jerusalem: Mosad Bialik, 1960.

Lawrence A. Hoffman and David Arnow, eds. *My People's Passover Haggadah*, 2 vols. Woodstock, Vermont: Jewish Lights, 2008.

Menahem Kasher. *Haggadah Sheleimah* [Hebrew]. Jerusalem: Torat Shelomoh, 1955.

Steven Luckert. *The Art and Politics of Arthur Szyk.* Washington, D.C.: The United States Holocaust Memorial Museum, 2002.

Shmuel and Ze'ev Safrai. *Haggadah Ḥazal [Haggadah of the Sages]* [Hebrew]. Israel: Karta, 1998.

Byron L. Sherwin and Irvin Ungar, eds. *Freedom Illuminated: Understanding* The Szyk Haggadah. Burlingame, California: Historicana, 2008.

Irvin Ungar. *Justice Illuminated: The Art of Arthur Szyk.* Chicago: Spertus Institute of Jewish Studies, 1998.

Katja Widmann and Johannes Zechner. *Drawing Against National Socialism and Terror* [German/English]. Berlin: German Historical Museum, 2008.

Ron Wolfson. *The Passover Seder.* New York: Federation of Jewish Men's Clubs, 1988.

Yosef Hayim Yerushalmi. *Haggadah and History.* Philadelphia: Jewish Publication Society, 1975.

Noam Zion and David Dishon. *A Different Night.* Jerusalem: Hartman Institute, 1997.